POWERING UP YOUR INNER BRAND

Defining the authentic 'you' for job and career

MARYLOU P. KAY

ISBN:149038555X
ISBN-13: 9781490385556

DEDICATION

To my dear husband, Bill, whose kind heart and good spirits sustain
me day in and day out.

CONTENTS

ACKNOWLEDGMENTS

I would like to acknowledge Allie Casey, longtime friend and author who gave me valuable advice, and Matt Domino whose knowledge of editing and publishing were a great help and comfort to me.

INTRODUCTION

I am passionate about branding, especially personal branding. The idea that a successful product is a recognizable brand is not a new one. The concept that a person's attributes and activities could add up to a brand which defines that individual, which captured my intellectual curiosity. It started with online recruiting, the job boards required you to build a profile, something like your resume, but it evolved over time. Enter LinkedIn which was described to me as an evolution of Plaxo. It was more than an online rolodex, it was a way to connect with people that you knew, worked with, and did business with. You could connect with those you might have lost contact with over time. You could showcase your skills by way of your profile.

That was almost ten years ago, and since then the internet connections field has exploded. Facebook has become a social innovator in countries where freedom of the press is a dream.
YouTube allows us to share every innermost memorable moment and lots of great 'how-to' information and instructions. Tweeting is a national pastime, and people are sharing details you would not have bothered to tell your friends about. Blog sites abound, with people expressing their opinions about everything and print job advertising is almost non-existent.

So if you're going to market yourself and your talents, you need to consider an online presence and that is what makes personal branding so important. Your online personality or brand must be congruent with your offline real persona. Your actions and your web presence must give a true and accurate representation of what you really are. When the person behind the Ziggs profile arrives for the interview, it should be the same person you see in front of you. What an opportunity to demonstrate my talents you think, but be aware that nothing is private and everything can be verified. *Once online, there for all time.*

A personal brand is more than a web presence, it's what you stand for, what you live by, the value you bring to any endeavor. That is why it's important to portray yourself accurately and share enough so that there is a context for your brand. It's tremendously powerful and at the same time presents serious challenges that every person must face. How do I handle less than successful career experiences? This is not about leaving a job off your resume; your profile exists in real time, so you will need to find a way to convey your story effectively.

Personal branding is interwoven with networking and job search. You can't really separate one from another, and so you will find many articles talking about interview skills and the process of job search. Nowadays, people are in a continual search mode. If they have a job they wonder how long it will last, and if they don't, obviously they're working very prodigiously to locate that next position. Networking is another continual activity. Whether you're building a personal business, or looking for vendors to hire for projects, you will be networking. As humans we like to do business with people we feel we know, and this is especially true with hiring.

There are those who we consider to be exemplars: people who embody their brand so completely they are indivisible. Whenever possible we will examine one of these Exemplars. We will also track the latest trends in hiring and interviewing along with ways to incorporate them into your personal brand and job search. Finally we will take a look at the dark side, negative branding, tarnishing your image, tragic brands and what we can learn from them.

Marylou P. Kay

I. NETWORKING AND JOB SEARCH

1. BRAND ENCOUNTERS OF A PERSONAL KIND

Some of the oldest questions asked by homo sapiens include 'who am I?' and 'What is my place in the world? The funny thing is that personal branding answers just those questions, very convenient. We are pelted with messages, 'brands' daily, so how does an able bodied professional leave their indelible mark in this morass of information?

A person leaves a mark by having their own personal brand, tried and true. It is the one thing that makes a person unique, a one of a kind specimen that will be remembered long after the sound bite ends. In order to launch a personal brand one has to come to terms with certain imperatives-who are you? What makes you different from others with a similar background? What do you like to talk about, read about? What are you good at? Everyone has a story, but you need to learn how to tell it in a way that is compelling. It also has to be concise, well written and fit into a format that can be easily published online, whether through a profile at a professional site such as Linked In, Ziggs, your personal blog, or website. People love stories.

When creating a profile, it has to have enough about you to show your individuality. Personal Branding can't be half-way, one must take the plunge. Of course it shouldn't be 'true confessions' but that reveal something meaningful others will relate to and interesting enough to remember you. Once a professional answers the basic questions, tells their individual story tingeing it with some humor and paints it on a background of current events and developments within their given field of interest, the 'story' comes to life, jumping off the page and into the reader's heart: voila, a personal brand is born.

2. BRANDING YOURSELF IN A CROWD

How do you make an impression during a networking event that looks more like a happy hour or a club scene? Well the writer happened to be in Coconut Grove last week at a networking get together, so here are some tips to get you through, brand intact.
The laws of attraction still apply, you must present yourself well; nothing too fussy but something that reflects your personality, preferably a business casual ensemble. It doesn't have to be flashy or designer, just tasteful attire that conveys the message you want to send.

Put your best foot forward: walk in, register. Be ready with your own badge in case they don't have name badges, and yes, put it on. You're here to network, which means meeting people who might connect you to other people and in that mix of contacts, you could discover someone who knows a person who refers you to an associate who may be aware of a business opportunity, or even a job. This is not for the faint of heart. Think of your specialty, your 'elevator speech', your 'pitch', that compelling story of you, experiences, skills, education. It's never an autobiography but a short, punchy story about you. So here you are at a restaurant packed with people, 3 deep at the bar, pizza hors d'oeuvres whizzing around you. Keep a smile on your face, look friendly, and be ready to start conversations with 'so what brings you to this meeting?' or 'are you a member of_____?' (Insert one of the sponsor organizations). I know they sound like lines you might have used back in the day, but you have to remember, networking is a little like dating, and you want to make the best impression in the shortest period of time. Being funny is one social leveling device: when people laugh, they relax and are open to hearing your story. Also, being humorous lets people know you don't take yourself so seriously, and that's essential to establishing rapport with others.

Now you should ask for what you want, but in a way that is subtle. Don't oblige people, just make them aware of your needs and how you can be of service to them. Reciprocity is key to this transaction. Remember, all you need is a new contact, a referral, but it has to be done with ease, grace, charm.

3. THE PITCH

What does the brand-savvy person do at a networking gathering when they've got 30 seconds to introduce themselves to a noisy crowd at a restaurant? Clear your throat and your head and get ready to put forth your best compelling 'elevator speech'. It should be pertinent, interesting, and invite people to come over and clamor for your business card.

That's a very short timeframe the writer was reflecting on during a recent networking event. It wasn't that large a group, yet how do you stand out and invite further inquiry from your audience. Once way experts advise is having an 'elevator speech'. Ok, so you've heard the term, but what does it mean?

Picture yourself on your way to a business meeting in a large building. You enter the elevator with a person who looks interesting, or maybe you know they are the head of the marketing department and you're a new grad, what do you do? You give them a 15-30 second 'pitch' which will say who you are, what you're looking for, and what you have to offer. That's it! Whoa, you say, that's what everyone is talking about? It's easy...well, no, it really isn't. That's because at that moment, in a pinch, you can't come up with some catchy, brief way to tell them about you in a meaningful way.

Now we're not talking about your life story, because even a six month old infant would need more than thirty seconds to explain all the new experiences they've had to date. No, we're talking about a succinct, precise 'pitch' that represents you the best you can, in a way that's understandable and interesting to the listener. Ahhh, the listener! Yes, it's important to think of the listener, to be sensitive to time constraints. If I'm at a networking event at a restaurant, I'm going to have some kind of beverage in my hand, and I may want to help myself to some of the appetizers being passed around or on a table in the center. I don't want to be stuck listening to your tale of woe about how you lost your job and are wondering what to do next. That's not networking.

Networking is smart, smooth, and sleek. It's hip, cool. You need to describe yourself and what value you bring in an inventive, energized way that will make people want to pursue a conversation with you, or even refer you to someone. It's a time to spark some shared interest or passion, to build a bridge to another person from an entirely different background and point of view. It's COMMUNICATING, which means there is person A sending and person B receiving the message.

Alright, you've got that part down, now how to formulate your message. Well I have some news, there's a website for that. It's called 15 second pitch.com and it helps you put your elevator speech together based on information you enter into a 'pitch wizard'. Yes, you enter your information and pop, out comes a little mini speech you can now use at those networking events, in airports, and even in an elevator.

Why does this work? Because we are all suffering from attention deficit syndrome. We can't pay attention for very long, and especially not if the speaker is lackluster, boring, tiring, and longwinded. "Brevity is the soul of wit" is my favorite proverb. It's in the fast repartee between two people that the most communication is happening. No one is there to listen to your detailed account of your last job, or your search for meaning in life! They are thinking, how does knowing you help them in some way? That is where you have to supply the reason. I promise you once you get this basic step down, and tune into the reaction it elicits, you'll have gone a long way towards articulating your personal brand.

Marylou P. Kay

4. MAKING SURE YOUR BRAND IS AUTHENTIC

When we talk about branding and careers, the idea is to find out what is authentically you and then tell your story in a compelling way so that others will relate to it. We are also hoping to get a job, a client, or a promotion. How realistic is that goal if we do not believe in what we are selling? If you are working for a company, but can't relate to their overall vision, or you don't believe in it, how can you possibly align your actions with it? Likewise, if you don't really know what you yourself are all about, how can you communicate that engagingly to your audience? You really have to be the brand, believe in the product or the company, or yourself in order to be truly convincing. I had a friend who used to say, "if I can't sell the company anymore, then I need to be gone". His idea was that if he no longer believed in what his company was trying to accomplish, their mission, then he would have to leave because it would no longer be meaningful to him. That's exactly how you maintain your authenticity; you must stay true to those ideas, concepts, visions that are real for you.

I was at a local meeting of the Greater Miami Society for Human Resources Management this past week and witnessed an authentic event. The topic for the meeting, which was a series of discussions and presentations, was diversity and inclusion. I always look at this topic as one that has a much wider context than having a good mix of people in the workplace, although that's a start. I always see it as a universal kind of truth, that our world is made up of so many different kinds of people, it's important to hear all of those voices, no matter how discordant. Of course, it's not always the case that the speakers embrace this vision, but this time it was. Don Mizell, Esq., music industry luminary and Grammy Winner, engaged the audience with a visionary chat "Diversity in an Expanding Universe".

One of the most impressive things about Mr. Mizell was that his vision of the world formed from watching television as a child, enabled him to see beyond what others might have thought of as restraints. As a boy, growing up in South Florida, Don imagined himself traveling the universe with Flash Gordon and Buck Rogers. He attended local schools here before moving on to Swarthmore undergraduate, and then Harvard Law School never letting the limitations of the outside world impinge on his grand vision. Mr. Mizell is an extraordinary example of nurturing that authentic voice within you and allowing it to take you to places you only dreamed of. It demonstrates how important it is to have a vision, and then go out and live that vision.

We can start by searching inward what is important to us. When we have sorted out our dreams and desires, we can put together a plan of how it is going to work, practical steps to get us towards that spaceship, or that brilliant career. Those steps become our action plan, but we can never lose sight of the vision that propels us. It's important to keep it close to you; maybe it's a personal mission statement that you review from time to time. You do not want to lose sight of what it means to you. This is a core issue for branding. Time and time again, we see people, companies getting distracted and falling off the path, diluting their brand; but it's by staying true to your own inner compass that your personal brand can stay the course.

5. NEW GRADS, NETWORKING, AND BRANDS

New graduates are a different kind of species. Still caught up in their world of friends, school and accomplishments, they find it hard to focus on the reality of getting a job. Sure we've heard this before, but these days, they are in a prime position to do some heavy networking. So instead of heading out to see the world, they need to be taking advantage of all the socializing around leaving school, parties, graduations, and get the word out that they are looking for a job.

A job you say, not a career? Well, no. The main objective is to land a job and it doesn't even have to be that prominent, special or difficult. You are not going to be spending the rest of your career there, so you should get something that would work for about a year and a half. After that, all bets are off. First of all, the company might change, you might change, and of course, the job will change. So why put so much thought into what the first job will be. No matter where you go, the first job will be an education, even if it's in what not to do on the job.

So, how are you branding yourself with this job? Aren't you tarnishing your brand by accepting something sub-standard? No, not if you look at it as a learning experience and try to take every opportunity to do new things. Once you're there a few months, you'll find you've assembled some pretty marketable skills. With time, you'll be able to look for something that suits you better, or change fields. It's a step by step process and at the beginning the steps are little ones. But guess what, you've already branded yourself as a winner- you got a job, you're handling responsibility and with a little time you can take on more.

Don't be afraid of volunteering or short term internships. Likely as not the company wants to try someone out before they commit to a full-time employee. So let them get a sense of you, and make no secret that you are actively looking and interviewing so they understand they're not your only option. Make sure to have a mentor, someone more established who shows you the ropes. This person, should you impress them, can be your best ally for the future. Don't forget, they have lots of contacts too, many of them outside the company. And maybe one day, just the right opportunity will come to you from a friend of a colleague you used to work with. Don't laugh, it's happened to me. It's all in the building of your personal brand

6. THE REAL THING: YOUR BRAND

We're hearing the unthinkable nowadays: a CEO of a prominent company stepping down because he didn't have the degree he said he had on his resume, a wedding photographer whose stolen portfolios were revealed overnight, leading her business website to be shut down. There are all kinds of examples of falsification out there, but why?

We talk about building your brand, your pitch or elevator speech, networking and putting your best foot forward. All these things are meant to showcase what you are, what you have accomplished and take you to the next level. The focus is on demonstrating the value you bring to any situation, including a new job. How can you be that personal brand you've built if it's not really you? The world is a very competitive place lately, so it's understandable if people want to represent themselves in a favorable light. The flip side is that we're all living in glass houses, our lives are an open Facebook, literally! Potential business partners and employers can find just about anything out about you by doing a 'Google search' of your name. Some companies have caused a fuss by asking for Facebook passwords from candidates so they can check on extracurricular activities. All of a sudden those wild college outings take on a more sinister cast. And all of the good things you've done, whether volunteering with the local youth group or meals on wheels, pale next to that one wild night with photos, or that degree you didn't complete.

Talk to an HR person, and ask them about what they have to do when they find an employee is not what they said they were, it's not good. People get fired their first week on the job because the reference check came back negative, or worse, no offer because the person had fake identification. It's inconceivable that people think they can get away with this, and yet very senior people are doing it. Most likely the degree wasn't really necessary to actually do the job, but it made the resume look better and once it's on a resume or an application, the individual has falsified a document. That has consequences.

To use that worn out phrase: honesty is the best policy. The most negative thing can be explained, and although challenging, it might be able to be understood and accepted. Social media and the web are extremely powerful tools in building your personal brand, but their power can be destructive if you are not who you say you are. This lesson is as pertinent for new grads as it is for seasoned networkers. Make sure your personal brand is the real thing.

7. BACKING UP YOUR BRAND

"A brand for a company is like a reputation for a person. You earn a reputation by trying to do hard things well." Jeff Bezos, Founder, Amazon.com

Let's think about that in terms of your personal brand. Are you trying to do hard things well? In this day of constant phone and texting, it's hard to believe anyone is concentrating, yet to really be good at anything, you must focus.

If we are distracted by texting, we can't drive, we all know that, but people are not aware of how that lack of focus affects other activities. What things are you doing that might distract you from building your A1 personal brand? Or, how are you damaging your brand by not doing hard things well? When you don't show up for a scheduled appointment, you have hurt your brand. When you give notice at a job, and then call in sick your final week, you have hurt your brand. You may think it doesn't matter, but it does. You could run into that same manager at another company someday who knows about your lack of accountability.

Ok, there it is: accountability. It is a very important word these days, and very little of it is floating around. Whether it's BP with the largest oil spill ever, or banks charging ridiculous fees, or Wall Street executives receiving obscene bonuses with 'bailout' money, no one feels obligated lately. But that is no excuse not to hold yourself accountable. No, you should demonstrate by your actions that you are responsible, reliable; your word is your bond. Your personal brand is your reputation; it's what people say about you when you are not around. If you let them down, or are not there for them, your brand will suffer.

Take a well-known brand, Ferragamo. They have offices here in Miami. They are known throughout the world for their fashionable, well-made leather shoes, handbags, and clothing. This brand was built through years of hard work, skillful design, using quality materials, precise tailoring, all to bring the customer the consistency of this product that is worth the Ferragamo name. Would all of your work measure up to the brand you are trying to create? It's not just about advertising yourself; it is about doing the quality work, whatever your field is, or being the dependable person that will reflect on your personal brand.

8. JOB SEARCH AND YOUR BRAND

We've heard it all, how to network, how to prepare your resume, the firm handshake and the direct eye contact. So what really works? Getting a job is hard work. It's very easy for companies to reject you and there are all kinds of reasons, but finally it comes down to one thing.

They didn't feel the trust and confidence that you were the person who could do the job and cause the least amount of disruption in the workplace. You would cause disruption? Well if you can't fit in, if you can't get along with the others in the office, and if you're not capable of doing the work: you're a disruption. That means they have to go back out and start the process all over again, and they don't like to do that. So they could be risk averse, taking their time until they find the absolutely perfect person. The trouble is, there is no perfect person, just like there is no perfect job. One person will do the job one way according to their skills and experience and another person will do it another way. This isn't an assembly line either. There is leeway in any job. Smart people know this and when they think the job is not so interesting, they find ways to make it more stimulating and creative. Those folks are usually the ones who get promoted too. Why? They're thinking of ways to improve the company, the tasks, the files, whatever is at hand. They can't help it; they do it almost without knowing that they're doing it. If you've ever had someone like this working for you, you know it's a pleasure because they anticipate what needs to be done.

And there's another magic word: anticipate. What's the definition of good service? Someone who brings everything you've asked for, or someone who anticipates what you want and brings it before you can even ask for it? That's true service. If we take that concept and put it into the interview scenario, what do we find? You must anticipate what that potential employer needs in someone who is going to do the job. That means research. Become a sleuth and find out about that employer. What are the dynamics of their industry? What are the challenges they are currently facing? When you read the job specification or the online posting, what words jump out at you? These are the questions you must answer for yourself. When you go into that interview, you need to portray yourself as the solution to their needs.

Let's look at an example. Janet is a computer programmer. She has been working for a small municipality, but then was downsized. Now she's looking to join the staff of a hospital. The hospital needs programmers, but Janet must demonstrate that she understands the way a hospital works, the kinds of programs they need, even how patient care is arranged. Janet goes to the hospital to observe the operation. She talks to people she knows and tries to connect with someone in the medical field. She reads articles about healthcare and learns the terminology used. She finds that a former classmate works at the hospital as a nurse and meets with her for coffee to talk about working at the hospital. When Janet finally goes in for an interview, she is able to show them that she understands how the hospital runs, and the kinds of projects she would need to do. She has some insight into what's expected from the hospital employees, and even some of the policies. When these topics come out during the interview process, the hospital administrators are impressed and feel that Janet will be able to fit in with very little training and orientation. Janet has made the transition, and demonstrated the value of her personal brand.

9. BRIDGING THE EMPLOYMENT GAP

Why do people continue to be unemployed when there are seemingly millions of jobs available? There are those who have given up, certainly, we have heard about them. They stop applying, or find part time work in an unrelated field to keep food on the table. We also hear about the snobs who say they won't hire anyone who is unemployed. I can't wait for those folks to be in the same boat and see how their impressions of the unemployed change. Then there are the skills gaps. Companies need people with updated computer skills, and good old fashion basics like reading, writing and arithmetic. You would be surprised how many college graduates cannot spell.

The first thing to do is to get acquainted with what employers need. This can be accomplished by reading the job postings on any of the larger websites. When you see a required skill that you do not have, avail yourself of online training, or local classes to learn the skills. Just the learning part will put you in a more positive frame of mind. In the metro Miami area, Spanish is a skill that is needed in many jobs. You can easily take language lessons in adult education or private language schools. If you are a native Spanish speaker and need to bring your English up to par, there are courses for that too in every school district.

In addition to understanding their needs, get familiar with the employers in your area and what types of jobs they tend to fill. The medical profession is booming with all kinds of ancillary jobs that alleviate the physician's heavy workload such as: medical assistant, physical therapist, physician's assistant. Courses in these fields are available both online and on campus. Bookkeeping and accounting skills are always in demand; just one course can get you closer to winning that interview. A number of people have tried consulting, appreciating the freedom of the consulting lifestyle. Bear in mind that you will have to be making contacts at all times for possible future projects.

Don't overlook volunteer activities that play well when you are questioned about employment gaps. Activities also keep you out there, interacting with people, telling your 'story', enlisting the interest of others and hearing about what industries are expanding in your area. There's nothing wrong with sharing with fellow job seekers. It gives you an outlet to express yourself in a 'safe' environment. Many times, it's through these people that you find out about new leads, so don't overlook that source.

I remember attending a job search network event some time ago, and the exchange of ideas that took place was very helpful. I made contacts that turned into friends over time. Shared adversity is a natural rapport-builder. It helps to keep up on local events. Which companies are opening headquarters in your area? What skills do you have that might be in demand? The employment gap is real, many jobs are open and companies are having a tough time filling them. It may require greater flexibility on your part as to where you live, or what salary you might accept, but there is employment waiting for you. Having a strong personal brand is an invaluable resource in times like these, but being aware of opportunity, where it might be and what it might require is the exact skill to help you narrow the employment gap.

10. HOW TO CONNECT AND GET A JOB

It's funny how we talk about being connected, we have friends, families, and our phones are filled with contacts. We go to events and participate in all kinds of activities, yet when we think about getting a job, we feel alone.

We dread making that call, imposing on someone, asking about a posting. In the last few weeks, I've attended some networking events. The great thing about the event sponsored by Greater Miami Society for Human Resources Management, Human Resources Association of Broward County and the local chapter of the Staffing Management Association was that it took place at Sun Life Stadium and had a speed-networking exercise. If you have not attended such an event, it has an MC who organizes the networking by giving instructions and blowing a whistle when it's time to change networking partners for the next introduction. It's fast-paced and active, forcing you to meet new people introduce yourself quickly, exchange 'elevator speeches' and move on to the next person. Similar to Speed Dating, it gives you a few minutes to get acquainted with someone, their background and what they are looking for.

When you think about it, this is exactly what we should be doing every day to make new connections and cultivate job prospects, but of course it would seem too forward to take every opportunity to let people know exactly what we need. Or our courage would fade at facing a total stranger and asking them for something that we want.

A second event was a bit kinder and gentler. Back on Track Network (www.backontracknet.org) is a faith based organization that offers support and guidance and connection to those who are unemployed. The meetings take place at churches in Miami Dade and Broward, and often there are speakers addressing the group along with some networking and sharing of job leads. The group at St. Bonaventura Church in Davie last Monday evening had the benefit of a speaker, Stephanie Stanford (Happy Ain't that Hard) who took the group through her story as well as some relaxation techniques and ways to get in touch with your inner fun-loving self. Once again the message is reach out and connect, and have fun doing it.

When we relax and open ourselves up to others, a sense of community comes about, a change happens within us and we no longer feel so alone, hopeless, forlorn. The very act of opening up and connecting has beneficial results on our brain waves. So why don't we do it more often? Why are we able to share on Twitter and Facebook things that we can't say to a colleague, or a business associate? Do we feel that awkward about expressing ourselves?

Well there's an easy way to resolve this issue, talk to people about it. Let them know what you would like, what you're concerned about, and ask them for a reference. In the society we live in, we do not like to obligate anyone, but sharing your story is just that, an invitation for someone to listen and understand. Make it clear that you don't expect them to take care of your problem, you need to show that you are willing to take that initiative, you're just asking for a guiding hand or thought, a gentle push. Is that so hard to do?

Think about this: we watch reality TV and the broadcastnews; we're always interested in hearing about the stories others, so perhaps your story can be that story that someone hears and relates to. That is what connection to others means. Sharing your story in an insightful way and letting them know you're open to ideas and suggestions gets the conversation going in a non-imposing way. Try it, you might just network your way to a new career.

11. INTERVIEW SKILLS

All kinds of people are looking for jobs these days, and happily some are even succeeding. There are all kinds of tips on dressing for success, the resume, the follow up, but this time we're going to focus on behavioral interviewing.

Alright, before you think I'm pulling the electrodes out to connect you, or shining bright lights on your face, I want you to understand what this is all about. You have nothing to fear but your inner truth! I guess for some of us that can be a little scary, but we're going to demystify it for you. There are all kinds of interview techniques: traditional questions with answers: "what are your strengths?", "where do want to be in five years?" We have all heard these questions and answered them at some time or another and sure it's fine to be ready for them.

However, let's look at something a little more probing. Behavioral event interviewing refers to a method of gathering data about your performance during an interview that involves discussion of exactly how you reacted in a given situation in the past. It is meant to demonstrate your past performance as an indicator of how you will do once you are on the job. This approach is supposed to get to the heart of how you will behave rather than just show off some nifty interviewing skills. After all we all know examples of people who are great interviewers, but terrible once they're on the job. With behavioral interviewing managers are hoping to overcome any of the false impressions that come with slick interviewers. Now if you're an average interviewer, chances are you're not going to shine like your well prepared counterparts, so how can you make the grade? Well, a good behavioral interview will give you that chance to show what you did and how fantastic it was for the company you did it for.

The tried and true method of preparing for a behavioral interview is to prepare by looking over your resume and your accomplishments and have a story that will display the skills you are looking to point up to the interviewer. The STAR method is the one most often used by placement firms and recruiters. It's an acronym to help you prepare: Situation, Task, Action, and Result. So you take a situation that you faced, perhaps it's an unhappy customer, and then you tell what had to be done (task), the action you took at the time, and finally the result of that action.

"Tell me about a time when you managed conflict effectively?" You would then reply, "I had a very angry customer in front of me, they were screaming. I checked their record and found that their account was put on hold erroneously. I got approval from my supervisor to correct it, and remove the hold; the customer was so delighted they wrote a note to my supervisor." In one sentence you've shown that you can calm someone down, take appropriate action while following the chain of command, and finally the customer was delighted enough to write a note recommending you. You can see why this approach is popular: it is non-discriminatory; it probes how you react in difficult situations and allows you the freedom to show who you really are during an interview. The idea is that an interviewer should feel like they are in the room where the incident is taking place, so you need to be as accurate and detail oriented as possible. In this way, you are taking your personal brand to a whole new level: that of authenticity. And that authenticity is what will get you the job.

12. BEHAVIORAL INTERVIEWING

We hear all kinds of horror stories about interviews these days, but you have to go through one in order to get a job. Here is a technique that has become very popular because it focuses on what you actually did on your job that was relevant to the current position available. First: What it behavioral interviewing?

Behavioral event interviewing refers to a method of gathering data about your performance during an interview that involves discussion of exactly how you reacted in a given situation in the past. It is meant to demonstrate your past performance as an indicator of how you will do once you are on the job. This approach is supposed to get to the heart of how you will behave rather than just show off some nifty interviewing skills. We all know examples of people who are great interviewers, but terrible once on the job. With behavioral interviewing managers are hoping to overcome any false impressions given by slick interviewers.

Second: How can you shine at behavioral interviews?

If you're an average interviewer, chances are you may not stand out like some of your counterparts, so how can you make the grade? Well, a good behavioral interview will give you chance to show what you did and how fantastic it was for the company you did it for. Why? Because the answers you give are uniquely you, not some made-up script or stock answers. You can't do well at a behavioral interview unless you share in depth about yourself.

Third: How will they know what to ask me?
Well, they don't. They ask you a general question and expect you to provide the specifics. For example they might ask you how you handled a difficult situation with a complaining customer. It's up to you to provide the setting and the details. You have to paint the picture, "it was in a busy doctor's office, and this patient had a crying baby who needed immediate attention... ". Once you've set up the situation, you explain how you were able to get the patient taken care of, the baby to stop crying, and the Doctor thanking you for your quick thinking.

Forth: Why do they use this style?
Behavioral interviewing is believed to be non-discriminatory, a fair way for you to show what you're made of and give in depth examples of how you get things done. As long as you did those very things, the interviewer will be able to see if you have the skill set to do the job, and they can tell if you are authentic.

Fifth: How can I prepare for this kind of interview since I don't know what they will ask?
Think about this word: STAR. In order for you to be a star you must describe the following:
Situation: What was the situation you were facing?
Task: What needed to be done?
Action: What action did you take?
Result: What were the results of that action?
This helps you remember what to focus on. It's simple and an easy way to promote your personal brand.

II BRAND EXEMPLARS

13. PAYING IT FORWARD

My friend Mike has a brand new job. He's heading up human resources for a successful firm in Atlanta. It wasn't always this way, some years ago he took a top job in the Miami Metro area only to be re-organized out of the company less than a year later. He spent some time soul searching and building a network: things he hadn't gotten to do while building his sterling executive career. He took time to get to know the needs of others. When he finally found a position, he had to relocate to Atlanta, but he had also acquired a new passion: networking. He realized that it is the key to staying on top of the job market, and even business opportunities. No one person can do it alone.

Mike's passion to share endeared him to many recruiters who would send him job postings for his network. This grew into a LinkedIn group, and the postings kept flowing in. He kept sharing them with all of his colleagues and networks. Mike got involved in public speaking, local not-for-profits and churches, and even found other partners in his quest to make sure the word gets out and that the leads be shared. If you're on Mike's list, he asks you to 'to pay it forward', that is think of others who are in need, pass on the information, and keep them topmost in your mind even when you're feeling low.

We all know that reaching out to others when we're down is tough, a test of our commitment, and yet it almost always leads to feeling better, and realizing you have value because you have something to offer. It's been talked about, and there have been some films, most recently "Cloud Atlas" plays on this theme, that we all need each other, that every good deed you do has an effect somewhere on someone. The movie also has other messages, but they key concept is trusting, offering something to someone else brings about a change.

Recently, we saw a story about Target where a customer had no money, and another customer offered to pay for their groceries. Others in line then offered to do the same for yet other people. Besides thinking cynically, "why can't I be on that line?" consider how viral the paying it forward idea can be.

Mike's new personal brand was social and community involvement, being sensitive to the needs of others. It brought him a whole new level of recognition and admiration which in turn opened up career opportunities. Before you start thinking it's a fairytale, think about how you remember that good turn someone did for you, recommended you, or shared an opportunity. You don't forget that person so easily, and you'll quickly return the favor should there be a chance.

Building your personal brand by paying it forward is real; it's opening yourself up to being generous whenever you can instead of always thinking what you're going to get out of it. It's gifting someone just because you feel like it, not for a reward but just because you want to. The action humanizes you and this is the core of a personal brand, since you're not an inanimate logo or a product. It's a way to demonstrate tangibly what your brand means. By the way, it does feel good, so there's an intrinsic reward to paying it forward.

Marylou P. Kay

14. FINDING YOUR VOICE

I was reading an article by Adam Lashinsky (editor-at-large, Fortune) about a writer he favors, Alexandra Fuller. She has written two memoirs about her life in Africa which Adam has found very moving. He laments not knowing that she had a more recent memoir about the demise of her marriage, and the irony he found was that it was Fuller's husband who had encouraged her to write 'the truth' after having many novels rejected by editors.

Now hopefully we don't have to go through a breakup to find our own true inner voice. Somehow, you would want it to jump out of you in some way and be apparent to all and highly original. I think these days with all this communication, texting, Twitter, Facebook, telephones, it is hard to find which voice is really your own. Did you ever think that the very issues you are speaking about come from someone else, or somewhere else?

So to be true to our personal brand, we have to scrape the surface and find out about who are we really and what we want to say. What do we want? What do we stand for? What is important to us? This kernel of truth then morphs into your elevator speech, your resume, and your entire modus operandi. It's the building block of the structure called YOU. Just as we each have a unique fingerprint, we have something within us that has a point of view that is of our own making. It is our perception of the world around us, our experiences, our talents, our virtues. It takes a little time to figure out what that is which is why young people might struggle with it. Of course I have seen young people who knew exactly who they were at an early age. I smile to myself, thinking about walking to school with my grade school companion, my best friend, and we were convinced that we were geniuses. Eileen and I didn't know what we were geniuses in, but nevertheless we knew that we were geniuses.

It is important to have a sense of self when you set out to define that inner voice. Someone who never finds it, might not be fully there, perhaps ghost-like, they are never sure what is at that inner core. When you build a personal brand, you need a strong foundation and a clear vision as to what makes it your own. Take some time, it does not have to be done overnight. Make sure that is the voice you take to interviews, the voice that writes the letters and emails and very important: your resume. Someone once said to me "the best author of your resume is you". No professionally written resume will have your unique voice. So be sure that your resume really reflects you in a meaningful way. It is one more building block of your personal brand.

15. BRAND EXEMPLAR: ROGER EBERT

Long before we even dreamed about personal branding, Roger Ebert forged a brand that evolved over almost fifty years of movie reviews in print, on TV and online and even on Twitter where he had 840,000 followers. Talk about adaptable. Roger Ebert started writing movie reviews at the Chicago Sun Times in the 1960's and by 1975 won a the first Pulitzer Prize given for movie criticism. Not one to rest on his laurels, he negotiated syndication with 200 newspapers, getting his message out to a broader audience. In 1975 he formed a partnership with his rival, Gene Siskel from the Chicago Tribune to pair up on a local public television show as an act arguing about the movies. This was pure genius because the interaction between the two was so compelling; they began to draw a national audience.

This was decades before thumbs became 'likes' on Facebook. The ability to banter about the movies generated discussion and enthusiasm in the viewers. The fact that these two guys looked like your neighbor or the guy at the office made them even more accessible. Suddenly, anyone could be a movie critic, and everyone was entitled to their opinion. It was the essence of democracy. In

1982 leaving public television the pair signed a contract with The Tribune Company and their show was syndicated with Siskel and Ebert getting a percentage of the profits. These were things that had never been done before. They signed with Disney in 1986 and the show evolved from "Sneak Previews", to "Siskel and Ebert at the Movies", to "At the Movies" and finally to "Siskel and Ebert".

In recent years even after fighting cancer and losing his voice, Ebert continued to thrive by writing books, appearing on TV and through his website, www.RogerEbert.com. He made use of technology in every way possible, taking to Twitter in 2009 and using a synthesizer when he could no longer use his voice. It wasn't just technology, but the sense of what people could relate to, what they were looking for that enhanced his offerings. He shared his passion and intelligence writing about movies and anticipated new trends in disseminating information. It's not just about talent, having a dynamic personal brand means staying present with what is going on in your industry, in business, in the world. Evolving is about following the flow of information and adding your own commentary, then considering how you can reach your audience. It has to be done in a way that doesn't offend yet invites discussion, that inspires caring and consideration. We have mentioned before the need to be authentic and Roger Ebert while being true to himself also pushed his personal brand envelope beyond anything that could have been imagined at the time he won the Pulitzer Prize back in 1975. Not bad for a newspaper hack.

16. WOMEN FORGING AN OLYMPIC BRAND

Is it just me, or is it true that in these troubled times of repressive regimes in world politics, the recent Summer Olympics games in London brought a ray of hope?   There were women participants from every single nation participating in the Olympics. It was the first time that women from 6 countries, Saudi Arabia included, were able to compete at the Olympics under the flag of their countries.

Let's take a look at some of our American compatriots and their inspiring successes. Of course we are familiar with the Williams sisters, Venus and Serena. Serena won the gold medal for singles tennis, beating Maria Sharapova. As if that weren't enough, she joined her sister Venus, and together they won gold for doubles tennis.   Misty May Trainor and Kerri Walsh Jennings with their three-peat, or a third Olympic gold medal for beach Volleyball! Of course, the Fabulous Five gymnastic team: first they win the team gold medal. Then we witness young Gabby Douglas winning the individual gold medal as Jordyn Wieber, who earlier in the week was disappointed because she did not qualify, cheering her teammate on encouragingly. And this is possibly the unique part, whether it's the rowing team, or the relay team, these women worked closely together, supporting each other through their ups and downs, successes and defeats.

This female sports brand is one that doesn't give up, doesn't abandon even in face of terrible odds and setbacks. Alex Morgan leads the women's soccer team to defeat Japan after having lost the World Cup to them in 2011. Allyson Felix won three medals, the first female track athlete to do so since Florence Griffiths Joyner in 1988. How about Candace Parker: she scored 21 points and 11 rebounds in the game against France to win the gold medal for women's basketball, the fifth time the women's basketball team has done this! Seventeen year old Missy Franklin followed in her idol Michael Phelps' footsteps winning five medals, four of them gold. Another amazing seventeen year old, Claressa Shields, won the gold medal for boxing, a sport that for the first time was allowed to be played by women.

Some of the stories are heart rendering: Gabby Douglas living apart from her family at a young age in order to train with a top coach in Iowa. Kayla Harrison won the gold medal in Judo despite having been abused by her former coach who is now serving time. Some stories inspire us such as Allison Schmitt, gold medal swimmer. Yes, she won five medals, but more impressive is how in the freestyle relay, Allyson swam the anchor leg, helping the U.S. team secure the gold, and then she again anchors in the medley relay as a replacement for another swimmer to win gold yet again! This was a world record.

The number of U.S. women competing outnumbered the men, and they out-medaled them too. In the many years since legislation ended discrimination in sports for women, this was a culmination of all of the efforts both of lawmakers and the women participating, many of them too young to remember how it used to be. Perhaps one of the most moving tributes to this brand is the new face of American sportswomanship: women helping and supporting one another in a way only they can do. The Olympics celebrates equality in athletics and fair competition, but our American women are celebrating a sisterhood that is moving forward with their own brand. That's a brand I can be proud of. Go USA!

17. BRANSON AND BRANDING

If you think about CEO brands, undoubtedly, Richard Branson comes to mind. Whether the early record company, or later the cheeky ads for Virgin Atlantic that touted a limo pickup as a part of the package, Richard Branson has always known how to do things the right way while making it look effortless and fun. Here is someone who did not finish school and did not have formal business training but somehow has managed to be known by most of the world not just for his brands, but for the 'joie de vivre' he projects. "We are a company that likes to take on the giants. In too many businesses, these giants have had things their own way. We are going to have fun competing with them." Now that sounds like something you want to be involved in.

According to a recent Burson-Marsteller survey, the CEO's behavior determined whether 95% decided whether to invest in a company. You only have to listen to Tony Hsieh talk about Zappos and their people to understand how important the demeanor and work ethic of the CEO is to the company and resulting corporate culture. What's even more surprising is that Branson keeps evolving. He recently started Little Red, a commuter airline that flies to Northern England and Scotland opening up a new market never considered by

Branson's competitors.

As if that weren't enough, his website is inspiring, full of ways to participate even in small ways, like adding captions on a picture, and of course demonstrating the corporate social responsibility, the concern for sustainability that we've come to expect from more buttoned up corporations. He has single handedly changed the paradigm of leadership. He's a leader, but also a great team member. Branson not only makes the world his playground, he's thinking People, Planet, Profit or new ways to develop economically for the good of underdeveloped countries.

So if you were a corporate brand, how would you model yourself? And in the same way, you can model your own personal brand to be outspoken, yet focused on a common good while yielding profits. It's the best of both worlds. Your mantra would be something like "I want to do good things, but also make a living at it, and make the earth better". If you can take such a core belief and turn it into a business, a career, you would have covered all the bases. It does require a consciousness of what might be valuable to people as well as what might be useful for the earth. In the middle of all that you need to enjoy it, since no one will appreciate a dull, lifeless brand. The very picture of Mr. Branson off on his latest adventure raises our spirits, and that too is the strength of his personal brand, the ability to engage our imagination thinking, 'what if?'.

18. SUPERHEROES AND YOUR BRAND

So if you were going to be a superhero, which one would you be? Are you the angry type who becomes a hulk? Seriously, who can't relate to that big green guy at one time or another when you're really mad? Or would you be all techno clad, like Iron Man? Then there's the old female standby, Wonder Woman, she was quite a gal in her day. A quirky favorite is Mighty Mouse, the little guy who overcomes all the odds. I mean, here he is a mouse, and yet he 'saves the day', you have to admire him. He may not be in the Avengers movie, but who knows, we may just see an updated version of our tiny hero popping up again. Of course Superman is the perennial constant, year in, year out, he 'wears' well, like his molded suit, his mysterious parentage, his super powers with one flaw-Kryptonite. It almost makes him human.

In recent years we've spent some time pondering Peter Parker's Spiderman, and the dark, moody Batman, played in turns by all kinds of leading men. Then of course there's the X-Men franchise, the Fantastic Four, we seem to want to believe in people who do good but have dubious wardrobe choices. We want someone who takes things seriously and cares enough to do something about it, puts their efforts into bringing about a change.

So wouldn't you like to show up as Superman at an interview? No, maybe not the tights, but 'you need that report done- no problem'. 'You've got logistics issues; I'll leap the tall buildings in a single bound way faster than FedEx'. We all want to show them our best side: how spectacular we are to make that fabulous first impression. At the core of the allure of the superhero is someone who is there when people need them desperately. A superhero is a person who comes up with a quick solution, who uses their power and strength to achieve good. That's not so different from what your average candidate would like to do. Job hunters whether experienced or new grads want to be able to soar into the skies and rescue the company from its current difficulties. And if you can do that, it's a part of what you want to tell them at an interview. If you've done your homework, you walk in ready to discuss how your contribution can assist them.

You talk about your expertise in taking care of that current challenge they're facing. You're targeting exactly what they need. That's the way you stand out from all the other regular folks who are interviewing. That's the way you come across like a superhero. So roll up your sleeves, and attach the cape. Build your own personal superhero brand –you might just get a job faster than a speeding bullet.

19. LEARNING FROM MOM ABOUT BRANDING

On Mother's Day, and besides being the worst day to go to a restaurant because they're overcrowded, we think about our mothers, or being mothers. We call to mind those nurturing qualities that make a mother, someone who not only bears children, but who raises them, teaches them. Our mothers confer to us all of the basic knowledge of our cultures and our family knowledge. They teach us love by loving us, and responsibility by taking care of us.

Mothering is something that society takes for granted, and we are always taken aback in the cases we do not see this instinct demonstrated. The mother who gives up her children, for example, we can't understand how that could happen. There are numerous discussions on the value of motherhood, including calculations of what a proper salary would be for all the work that goes into it, but that comparison is rather surface. It's so much more than just the cooking, the wash, and the chores. I was at a doctor's visit some years ago, and the young doctor had just lost his mother. What he said to me remains with me still, "your mother is your cheerleader, when she's gone, there is no one who will celebrate your achievements the way she did." Aptly put.

It's exactly what we can learn about personal branding from our mothers. Take for example your 'elevator pitch' that fifteen to thirty second summation of what you are about. Even with handy websites like www.15secondpitch.com, we're at a loss to come up with exactly the right way to present ourselves to that stranger we encounter in an airport, a lobby, or an elevator. Yet, I'm sure if we think about how our mother might explain us, we come near to the perfect elevator speech, because mom could sum it up pretty quickly. Think about those things she told you about yourself, from her perspective. You can also think about how she might describe you to her friends.

In short, the brand our mother gives us is our first brand. Of course we grow and mature, we pursue an education, we learn from our experiences, but it's truly this core of what we are about which she understood so well that allows us to define ourselves in terms of our relationship to the world. Exploring within and acknowledging those things about you will lead you to find just what makes your personal brand unique. How did I know that? Your mom told me.

20. YOUR LIFE: SUMMATION OF A PERSONAL BRAND

We talk about branding and how to network, find jobs, and build a personal reputation based on our actions, accomplishments, interests. There is no greater proof of an admirable personal brand than that of a life well lived and communicated to those around them. A person who stands for something, and when that life has run its course, those close to him can remember with caring fondness what that brand was all about because it was made abundantly clear every day through their actions.

One such person comes to mind, H. Michael Torlone, who passed away last week. No, Mike will not make national headlines, he lived and gave example through his works and passes unheeded by the world at large, but for those of us who knew him, he was larger than life. Mike was born in 1923 in Boston, obtained his education and went to work in a family business at a young age. He had the gift of a beautiful bass voice and met his wife, Rosemarie, singing in a choir. A music lover, their marriage of fifty seven years was a model symphony. Two strong individuals, raising children, moving to Florida and building businesses, they were never far from their faith and the music that gave them sustenance.

Michael was devoted to his family, helped his church, his community, his friends. The services held included moving tributes from his son, his friends and fellow choir members. Everyone shared a special way that Michael had touched their lives, with knowledge of finances of which he was very astute, to music and opera, to food and good company. The group was regaled with stories both humorous and touching, each one detailing some special gift that he had shared with them at a time when they most needed it.

And this is emblematic of a strong, meaningful personal brand. People come into our lives and in one way or another at that very moment when we need them; we receive the wisdom we ourselves have missed. The writer experienced this very gift: Mike gave me the courage to take control of my finances at a time when I felt lost and overwhelmed by the complexity of them. His discipline and patience in these matters is legendary, and I am grateful to have received the benefit of his expertise.

As we move through our lives, building our own brand, it serves us well to think about what legacy we leave behind us in the ways we have been attentive to those around us and their needs. Michael Torlone was a quiet man, some would even say shy, yet he listened, and looked you in the eye and offered you what he could in a very basic and honest way. This is the kind of brand we can only hope to emulate through our own contributions. He is sorely missed.

21. THE IRON LADY

This past year has seen the passing of an iconic world leader, Margaret Thatcher. Often called the 'Iron Lady', this label defined her strong, unyielding leadership at a time when it was most needed by her country and by the world. This sobriquet or title is a perfect example of what Verne Harnish (Gazelles Inc.) calls the one word or phrase that defines what you are all about. Mr. Harnish tells us that for most of us career success will be non-existent if we do not create this phrase and then live it.

More than an elevator speech, this is one or two words that create your public persona to indelibly engrave you into the minds of the public thereby solidifying your personal brand. Certainly this past week has seen the passing of one who exemplified this theory. Consider the 'Iron Lady'. This name was given to Mrs. Thatcher by Captain Yuri Gavrilov in 1976 in the Soviet newspaper Red Star. It calls to mind a woman firm in her beliefs who does not avoid difficult situations. Margaret Thatcher was smart, politically astute, and not afraid to assert herself or live her convictions to the fullest. She was resolute and determined, not one to back down from a fight. Mrs. Thatcher provided leadership to the United Kingdom at a time when it most needed it and furnished the example for others to follow.

Notably, the United States under Reagan's leadership added the complement needed to exemplify the personal responsibility and hard work that were the cornerstones of her brand. Strength under fire is what this 'Iron Lady' projected when the Falklands Islands were invaded in 1982. More recently, the so named movie with actress Meryl Streep(another example of a strong personal brand) brought to light once again how extraordinary Margaret Thatcher's accomplishments were for those times, and even for today. We do not easily find contemporary examples of this kind of solid, forceful leadership. Verne Harnish tells us that being crystal clear about who you are opens the door to numerous interesting opportunities.

Margaret Thatcher exemplified this by standing her ground and rallying the British Empire around her at a time when it was most needed. It brings to mind another great lady of times past, Queen Elizabeth the First. She defeated the invincible Spanish Armada and forever changed the map of the world. These heroic role models chose their defining word and stuck with it, every action embodying their personal brand.

22. MALALA: THE UPLIFTING BRAND OF A YOUNG WORLD LEADER

A sixteen year old girl addressed the United Nations recently. Malala Yousafzai, a Pakistani school pupil and education activist from the town of Mingora in the Swat District of Pakistan's northwestern Khyber Pakhtunkwa province spoke to the world about the one thing she wants to accomplish. She was born in 1997, four years before the 9/11/2001 attack on the United States, but this young lady knows about war. She was shot by the Taliban for advocating education for girls. The Taliban, those so-called warriors who would let a school full of girls in a burning building die rather than come into contact with an unmarried female.

The diminutive Ms. Yousafzai in her pink head scarf looked more like a 'quinceañera' than a world leader, but her courage, determination and will to survive has catapulted her to the world stage, she is a leader and an inspiration to all women and freedom lovers around the world. She may become the youngest person yet to win a Nobel Peace Prize, and it will be well deserved for calling attention to the need for education in so many developing countries.

Her words are those of a leader: ""Let us pick up our books and pens. They are our most powerful weapons. One child, one teacher, one pen and one book can change the world. Education is the only solution." Impressive from anyone but especially a sixteen year old Pakistani girl from a small village who had the courage to speak out at the age of eleven, and who suffered for that at age fourteen when she was shot in her head and neck on her way home from school last October.

For this tenacious young lady, her only desire is to speak up for the rights of girls and all young people about the right to an education. Malala handed a petition to the UN Secretary General Ban Ki Moon signed by four million people calling on the UN members to finance teachers, schools and books to meet the need for education. She stressed the need for all children to be able to go to school:
"The terrorists thought that they would change my aims and stop my ambitions but nothing changed in my life, except this: weakness, fear and hopelessness died. Strength, power and courage was born."

This is indeed the voice of a leader. We can make no mistake about what Malala stands for and we can take a lesson from her intrepid spirit. Her cause having taken on a life of its own, causes us to take stock of our own brand, what do we stand for? What is the one thing we would like to accomplish? Remember that no goal is too small, even if it's that of enabling a child to get an education. If we apply this to our career and our life, is everything we present to the world related to that inner truth? We have spoken in the past about true identity, finding your voice; Malala Yousafzai has found her voice. What is yours?

III POP CULTURE

23. MAKE YOUR BRAND RESONATE

First of all it's your brand, you: that unique ball of wonderfulness that you must convey to the rest of the world. We've talked about how your mom might put it. So with those thoughts as your guide you can now try internalizing those ideas into expressing yourself in a way not done before. Your goal is to have an authentic interaction with others that will stay with them, something that explains by your actions what you are all about. So here are my five personal favorites:

1. You had me at 'hello': Try thinking of every person you meet as the next biggest treasure in your life. People will relate to that openness and positive attitude you're projecting. And I don't mean just the people you think can help you, but all those other people you meet along the way.

2. Be a good listener. Everyone is trying to communicate what's important to them. Make it about them, not you and really listen without judgment or reaction. What are they really trying to tell you but not verbalizing? Internalize Mr. Spock by uttering "how interesting" or "fascinating" when prompted for a response.

3. Stop saying "but..." For example, "Jane, I really like that new

business proposal, but…" After that, they won't remember that you liked the business proposal, they will only think of what came after "but…" So stop saying it. Hold off on any comment that might be perceived as a negative and make yourself open up to the possibility being presented to you.

4.   Go out of your way to help someone. Whether it's a colleague, a family member, a stranger you meet, do something out of the ordinary and write a recommendation, or send a referral. You will feel good about yourself which should be enough, but word of those good deeds gets out there quickly and you will find people drawn to you.

5.   Put yourself in their shoes.   This is especially true with interviewing for just as you are nervous about going to an interview, the recruiter is concerned they won't get it right, won't fill the job, and won't meet their deadline. Take a minute to recognize that the other person is a human being who has needs too. This is a great leveler with people and leads to a more genuine exchange.

So there you have it, the five things that will make people remember you, make your brand resonate with all who meet you. You will feel less alienated and friendlier, more dynamic and open to new opportunities. After all, you get one chance to demonstrate your personal brand.

24. DELINEATE YOUR BRAND WITH JOB TYPE

Lou Adler, noted author (<u>Hire With Your Head</u>, Wiley, and <u>The Essential Guide for Hiring & Getting Hired</u>,) simplifies job search and self-definition beautifully with his premise that there are only four kinds of jobs in the world. As Lou puts it:

> Everything starts with an idea. This is the first of the four jobs – the Thinkers. Builders convert these ideas into reality. This is the second job. Improvers make this reality better. This is the third job. Producers do the work over and over again, delivering quality goods and services to the company's customers in a repeatable manner. This is the fourth job.

Can it be this easy? Well, we probably are all combinations of two of the types, but yes, it can be. What are you good at? Are you the one coming up with that breakthrough idea leaving everyone wide-eyed with confusion and disbelief? Well, you're the Thinker. You like new projects, taking the impossible and making it possible.

Do you like to roll up your sleeves and take the idea, turning it into a program or a system, or a product? Then you are a builder and you are happiest turning concepts into creations. Or maybe you like to look at what exists, and make it better? Then you are an Improver.

You have strong analytical skills and are able to take the process to a new level. Finally, are you able to make the product and deliver it to the customer's satisfaction in a consistent manner? Well, then you are the Producer, the person getting it done time and again.

Adler says that most of us are a combination of two of the four job types. He feels we should get that part right and not slot ourselves (or be slotted) into the wrong types of jobs. Ponder the thinker who's asked to make the same thing consistently; it's just not going to work. Or consider the Improver who's asked to come up with a completely new concept? This may not come about at all.

As we've mentioned in times past, it's important to know your strengths, preferences and play to them instead of trying to be something you are not. If you've had unprecedented success churning out quality products and are asked to take an unproven concept to market, you will either be incredibly stretched, or painfully frustrated.

Thanks to Adler, once we know our job type, then we organize our job search strategy, our resume, and our networking in order to go after the optimal job. And by the way, that job type preference added to your unique skills and experience, becomes your personal brand.

25. YOUR GLOBAL/DIVERSE BRAND

Feeling global? We talk about it, but do we put ourselves in the shoes of others. It's the essence of human nature to think of our own agenda first. We're hard-wired that way. And I'm not going to get all dreamy eyed and say what about the greater good, because there's ample evidence that not many other people are thinking about that. So I'll approach it from the pragmatist's point of view: it simply makes things easier.

Resolving issues without that contentious process of point/counterpoint is shorter and more efficient. Yeah, I know, saying it and doing it are two different matters. But if you can think about your interactions with global colleagues, how much did it help when you finally listened to their needs, or showed them that you could empathize with their plight. It softens that resistance that's naturally going to be inside them, because after all you're from 'corporate' and by now they know you're not here to 'help'.
So don't pretend to help, just get in there and anticipate their needs.

Let your curiosity drive you to coming up with solutions and compromises. They know you might be a step up in the decision process, but you can also let them know the difficulties you're facing so they can understand why you might be asking for something, or advocating something.

From there, it's a process of getting to know and trust, that can take some time, but it will lead to greater cooperation on both sides, and that will get the job done. Remember that unspoken resistance can kill a program faster than any management disapproval. You really don't want them saying 'yes' when they mean 'no way!', that hurts both of you. Get next to them, feel their issues, and show them that you're trying to make a difference. When you come out there with your vulnerable honesty, you'd be surprised how engaged they become. That just might be human nature too; most folks don't want to kick a dog when he's down.

We talk a lot about diversity; we have for some time at least in the U.S. But do we take it to the next step? Our country is on the surface welcoming to diverse cultures, religions, races, lifestyles. We have laws that protect people in the workplace, in securing loans and housing, but of course there is still a lot lacking in true acceptance of others who are different from ourselves.

In the past months we have witnessed needless conflicts over differences, acts of violence and terrorism, ongoing wars, or reckless attempts at countries trying to prove themselves by shows of force with dangerous weapons. And we wonder, what does this mean? Why does it have to be this way?

So it's no wonder that we want to consider a multicultural brand-a personal brand that can reflect who we are, but also project who we want to be. And we want to be that one who can welcome all kinds of cultures, experiences, lifestyles. I don't have to let those specific things define me; I can define myself as someone who is open to others whose ways are different from mine.

This might mean that when I'm meeting new people I don't let them define me narrowly, yes, maybe I'm originally from New York, but I've lived in other places and speak several languages and I enjoy being in multicultural environments. I respect those differences and try hard to bridge them whenever possible. It can be as simple as listening, or reacting with curiosity rather than judgment and disdain.

One of the worst things we can do when meeting new people is to assume they are coming from the same point of view. You can immediately alienate someone to the point where anything you say will not be considered. We all know situations when meeting an obnoxious person, we now dismiss anything they say as erroneous. What if the way you represent yourself makes people think of you in that same way: dismissively. Not fun, right?

A wise friend once told me that the secret of getting along with in-laws was to pretend you were an anthropologist encountering a 'new' tribe. Instead of evaluating their words and actions, study them with curiosity, making a mental note or two. It's a very helpful way to experience others without judging, so I would recommend that when meeting new cultures, you observe and try to discern what is going on, how they communicate. Is what they are saying really what they mean? That is how you begin to create that open mentality, considerate and respectful of the differences of others. It is the way that most allows you to learn. Ability to think differently and learn is a particularly useful skill. If enough people practiced it, we might actually reduce conflicts in the world, and enjoy the diverse tapestry of humanity as a backdrop for our own personal brand.

When you are interacting with global cultures, it's important to come up with solutions that fit in with what is innate to that culture. So whether you are traveling internationally or interacting with an international workforce here in the U.S., the respect for that culture is essential. You may have an agenda, some plans you need to carry out, but you do have a choice in how to carry them out, and this will come from a well-developed global perspective. Sometimes your good intentions in respecting the local practices can be at odds with what the team at corporate expect you to do. You are adapting the brand, but company may find that it's harder to do things in a different way in each country or location. It's complicated, hard to administer. In many cases the corporate folks may not have been out in the field so to them, they are not real people with needs that are quite different from what exists at the head office and these people are making the decisions.

And that is just a shame. A case in point is the example of my colleague Amparo, hospitality professional. She has assisted various luxury hotel chains in opening new hotels throughout Mexico, in Cancun, Mexico City, Cabo San Lucas, and Mazatlan. A trained psychologist in addition to being brilliant human resources professional, Amparo works closely with a general manager to bring the dream of the exquisite luxury hotel into reality, with all the steps in between. That means the selection, the hiring, the training, and policies all have to be created. A hotel is a lot more than a group of buildings and pools, it's an ambiance that is created through top notch service provided by employees who have been selected and trained. Many times in these distant locations, finding the right individuals with training is a challenge. Putting together the right team and training them to perform in a coordinated fashion is science, art and a little bit of magic, but when it comes together, it's a beautifully orchestrated symphony of service.

Amparo had returned to the company a few years after leaving it hoping to recreate the kind of project she had been successful at achieving in the past. The resort hotel chain had evolved in its thinking, trying to be more formulaic in how it brought about that 'magic'. So Amparo had to recruit online, even though the candidates in this area of Mexico do not have access to computers.

They had to pass a psychometric test online before they could be interviewed. And when Amparo tried to explain the difficulties to the non-Spanish speaking HR executive based in London, she was told no variations were allowed. Of course it took longer to get the staff in place, and there were delays in training the new recruits…and finally Amparo moved on, not surprising in hospitality.

If your personal brand is one of multicultural understanding, the inflexibility of a company that refuses to adapt to local circumstances is frustrating. If employees in Europe can undergo the online tests, why can't a rural Mexican population do so? And that is the heart of matter, being multicultural is not a rubber stamp. Just like a personal brand cannot be the same as another. Your brand is an indelible mark on the world of what you stand for. No matter what the situation, or the industry, or the company, your brand is in tune with local practices while embodying a universal intelligence and acceptance. You understand how people get hired in Mexico, or Cambodia, or Slovakia. You research them, how they relate to authority, and what skills they must be taught. Now if only multinational organizations would absorb the practical local knowledge and share it with the chiefs at HQ, it would go a long way to address what they were trying to accomplish.

Marylou P. Kay

26. MILLENIALS CHARTING NEW BRAND TERRITORY

The Presidential debates last fall drew our attention for many reasons; the candidates have very distinct brands. On the one hand you had Romney, successful businessman, Republican, wealthy. On the other hand the incumbent, Obama, who had four difficult years with not very much to show for it. It's not that he hasn't tried, but there's been too much to take care of at once. The lack of focus is lethal. We have a healthcare bill that is confusing to everyone, and frightening to small businesses who may just give up offering health insurance. We have continuing high unemployment, something that's unacceptable here in the land of the freedom to work. How it would play out in November was hard to determine at the time. A lagging Romney looked like he was catching up. Obama was ahead and popular, but some of his past false steps made people ask themselves: am I any better off than I was four years ago?

This means that many of us are still looking for jobs. We may be underemployed, we may be consultants, we may be new grads, but all we really want is to get a job. Being true to my own personal brand as a consultant, I do enjoy coaching and counseling people to get jobs. I believe in going after that job for there still are jobs to be found. Part of why we invest in our personal brand is to ensure we will have adequate choices for positions. As a part of a committee on

Workforce Readiness with the Greater Miami Society for Human Resources Management (GMSHRM), I went to Job Corps in Homestead to address students on the skills needed to get jobs. This is always a tough situation: you are trying to give hope to a group of people going out for the first 'real' job after getting a degree or a certificate. You want to motivate them to get out there while giving them all the tips you can provide in order for them to make a smooth transition to the adult world. You know that it's not going to be easy, this is not for the faint of heart, yet you don't want to frighten them either where they fall into despair. At such a young age, despair is tragic.

Armed with my trusty presentation and two cups of coffee, I set out to give them my wisdom in the best way I could: give them the benefit of my experience, even some of the tough things. I wanted them to know that you can get through rejection and adversity. I wanted them to put themselves in the shoes of the interviewing companies, I wanted them to prepare in a way that would surprise the hiring managers. I also wanted them to feel comfortable in their own skin as they went out to that interview, to allay their fears and tell them that the interviewer is nervous too, that they are human.

They were a lively group despite having listened to other presentations before mine; they maintained their enthusiasm and curiosity. They believed what I told them and took it to heart. They absorbed the wisdom and courage I tried to impart in my own way, in order to get ready for their turn. I know that many of them are going to be successful. You could see the light in their eyes. I was tapping into the dynamism of this "millennial" generation: they are strong; they are not going to take things lying down. I felt confident in their ability to somehow overcome the odds, and get to that place they wanted to go.

If a generation has a personal brand, I think this one is determination. They are open to hearing what happened before by the older generations, but ready to go out and do it their own way on their own terms. Inspired by that, I wondered if it really mattered who became President. This generation is going to get fed up with the runaround that Congress is giving the American people: watch out as they step up to make the necessary changes. Now that's a brand for the future of the country.

Marylou P. Kay

27. CHANGING YOUR BRAND DIRECTION

With workshops touting, 'Talent trumps experience every time', meaning a talented person can figure out more things than someone with years of experience, we start to wonder is it time to just back away? I'm taking nothing away from talent. A talented person is one you might not have to spend much time in training, they understand right away. It's a pleasure to work with someone like that. But there are people who have years of experience to offer when the going gets tough, and they can figure out a way to resolve a thorny problem. Doing the same thing day after day for twenty years may not require originality or innovation, so again I understand why a talented person seeing the problem with new eyes for the first time will come up with a whole different approach. I just don't what to discount what a seasoned individual brings to the table.

Where do you stand in this continuum? I believe we need a mix of people in the workplace. In fact, I think it's the diversity of the mix that fosters greater innovation and achievement. We need both young achievers and tenured individuals who have faced a crisis or two in their experience. If the two can collaborate, the results are astonishing.

So when is it time to just walk away, like Hillary Clinton, Tim Geithner, or Jodi Foster? They are hardly 'old' in the modern sense of the word; in fact they may be at their peak of competence. Perhaps they are starting a new life, or going into new careers. Maybe they are taking a break to reconsider their choices up until this time? They are going to change their personal brand into something different than it was before.

At some point, we look at our personal brand and what it has come to mean to us, to our employers, families and friends, and we decide that we want to do something different. It could mean we take a hobby or pastime and turn it into a second career. It could mean we no longer want to put in the 40-50 hours a week in that corporate job and desire a kinder, gentler existence, possibly working part time. I doubt that Tim Geithner is going to be a greeter at Wal-Mart, but there are things he could be doing that would not be as 'taxing' as his former role.

The question that seasoned individuals often face is the surprise of others who cannot understand that they might want to slow down and smell the flowers. Some friends recently sold their home and possessions and bought a trailer that will enable them to travel the country. One spouse has a financial consulting practice that he can manage 'on the road', the wife just wants to see things she's never seen before whether it's Washington D.C. or Yellowstone National Park. Many friends questioned this new direction; others were downright envious and wondered if they too could take the same steps. What's a life for anyway?

The other thing that people who examine potential changes in schedule and lifestyle face is the lack of understanding by companies, bosses, hiring managers. How many times has an individual been told, 'you're overqualified for that job' when all they want to do is exercise their skills and talents, get paid and go home at 5 pm every night. They no longer want to climb the career ladder. They are not interested in proving how talented they are. They do want to contribute. They do want a paycheck, but maybe they'd like a few less headaches. Why is that so hard to accept?

Allowing your personal brand to age gracefully means that the choices that were suitable five and ten years ago, are no longer appealing. You might accept a position that former colleagues feel is beneath you, yet you are completely satisfied with it and enjoying life. Others may doubt the person's sincerity. Somehow this person must be looking to grab the top job, or jump ship to another firm at the first chance. It's very hard to convince a younger overachiever that you are fine with the here and now, because it fits with your overall lifestyle.

Can others allow us to pursue these new options? I think we need a new paradigm. As a society, we need to give ourselves permission to move in different directions, to the side and not just up; and take away the stigma on those not wanting to be so hard-charging and ambitious. Let's agree to a new kind of diversity, a diversity of direction, a brand that is allowed to grow past the hurdles of yesterday into something that is rewarding and no less our personal choice.

Marylou P. Kay

28. KEEPING YOUR BRAND AGE NEUTRAL

Grandparents Day is September 9th, a holiday recognized since 1978. Although many of you think of your grandparents as kind older people who can spoil you in a way your parents can't, being a senior citizen today is a lot more complicated than it's ever been. For starters, grandparents are working. They are active members of the workforce and this trend seems to be continuing in light of recent economic conditions. Maybe you remember a time when your Grandmother was at home baking cookies or knitting, but not anymore. They may be working out of financial necessity or they might have a career that they are not ready to give up. They may be temporarily unemployed and searching for a job, trying to stay up on current trends. They may even need your help in figuring out the I-phone, or the newest laptop.

Many seniors are active and making a difference in the lives of others. We just recently witnessed an exciting speech given by President Clinton at the Democratic National Convention. People are asking: did he steal the show? He certainly made an impression. Not to mention Clint Eastwood's discourse with an empty chair at the Republican National Convention, he is still very active and not just in films. We are witnessing an older generation continuing to make a contribution, and refusing to be thought of as 'over the hill'. So how can we apply that to a personal brand?

With the current multi-generational workplace, it's important to find a middle ground, to fit in without disregarding your wisdom gained over the years. An older person does have something to offer, but it has to be in a way that others can relate to. There is an expression from Adlai Stevenson "it's not the years in your life, but the life in your years that counts". If you come across as someone who is not open to new ideas, or you dismiss anything new as something you tried unsuccessfully long ago, people are not going to share information, or even come to you with questions. This is a shame, since an older person does have a lot to offer. They have experienced many setbacks and have been able to overcome them. If this could be shared with others, how many obstacles might be easily surmounted? But the sharing has to be non-confrontational, and couched in terms that reflect today's sensibilities.

This age-sensitivity extends to the over 40 job seeker. It is important to demonstrate that you are able to do the job and are familiar with all the latest components, including Microsoft Office, which means you can create your own memos and reports, because that's what businesses require: people, who can manage, function as a team member and write their own reports. It's important to show respect for those who are younger and less experienced. It is no longer an accepted fact that the older person has more to offer, the millennial generation has been contributing many advancements in business, a look around at the CEO's of some the most successful businesses will offer ample proof. But of course there is something to be said for the wisdom gained through difficult experiences. A baby boomer may have to search deep within to find their self-worth, their emotional intelligence to offer it to others.

Another way for the 40 plus or 50 plus job seeker to create their age neutral brand is to stay engaged: in life, in your field, in the world. An active mind and spirit can assist seniors to project a youthful impression. It is very refreshing to interact with someone who has all of this knowledge and experience and is still passionate about what they still want to accomplish and eager to share this with others in an exciting way. Age does not have to stand in the way of your career if you present it as an asset rather than seeing it as a liability. So turn the tables on those Millennials and offer them the benefit of your successes and your mistakes. Be open to learning new things, it will make you feel youthful and project a wise, age neutral brand.

The Ladders.com is an excellent job search site for senior level positions. This job board has grown considerably over the ten years it's been in existence, but perhaps one of the best features is the advice mails you receive from Marc Cenedella, Founder and Executive Chairman. Marc is passionate about job search and always thinking about what the applicant is experiencing out there in the cold cruel world of key word search and online application systems' black holes.

Marc is also not afraid to tell you like it is, and try to constructively help you through the tough spots you face, such as handling the 'age question' gracefully. A recent article is no exception. What he is telling you is that you cannot blame interviewers and recruiters for age discrimination no matter how subtle it may be. You have to put yourself in their shoes, they are thinking about whether you will have the energy to get the job done, the openness to learn new things, cooperate with colleagues of all ages, and take direction from those who are younger. Flexibility is the single greatest asset you can demonstrate to a potential employer.

So how can we cultivate this? First of all it doesn't mean that you adapt inappropriate jargon or attire, you don't have to be young. What employers are looking for is the open-minded willingness to learn that is often found in young people who have not had years of experience to affect their point of view. We all know someone older than ourselves who demonstrates this kind of excitement and passion about what is going on in the world who can vividly describe how they see their role in the midst of the changes: that is what employers are looking for. They love when someone is emotionally mature, conscientious, willing to roll up their sleeves and get in there and also share their vast knowledge. This would not be the kind of person who will suffer age discrimination, because they are demonstrating an abundance of value.

That expertise, those times you made mistakes and learned how to do it better, that is very useful for an employer. If you couple that with a willingness to adapt to new technology and keep up on what's going on in the world (and I ask you, what is the alternative?) then you will have an extremely valuable mix of skills coupled with a positive attitude that will not escape the eyes of a sharp recruiter. Uncle Marc tells us we have to 'show' these things, meaning give examples of situations and how we resolved them. But that's just good interviewing skill, as the tried and true STAR method shows us (Situation Task Action Result). Nonetheless, be ready, it's exactly what is going to give you that personal brand of *'insightful, determined professional of an indeterminate age who is able to do anything'*. Not exactly the phrase you want to put on your resume, but apropos just the same.

29. IMPROVING YOUR BRAND WITH EQ

Emotional intelligence or EQ became popular in the 1990's. There have been many proponents of this new kind of intelligence. Daniel Goleman has been widely recognized for his approach and his television special on PBS is still a classic primer on how your emotions are tied to the more primitive part of your brain.

Recently there have new additions to the literature, notably Travis Bradberry and Jean Greaves with their book Emotional Intelligence 2.0. There are lessons we can take away from EQ to enhance your personal brand. We've all been in interviews where they ask us about how our colleagues perceive us, or how our subordinates relate to us. They are trying to find out how we come across in most human situations. How do we handle stress? Do we have a problem with authority? Do we just react? Or do we actually pause and try to manage our emotions? Self-awareness leads to self-regulation. If we become aware of how our emotions affect us, what pushes our buttons, we can better handle the situation.

Emotional intelligence can assist us in most social situations. Some of the new techniques include really listening to others as they speak and trying to decode the non-verbal messages that they may be sending with their body language. When we have conversations oftentimes, we are just waiting to make our next point, rather than focusing on the other person. Being aware of the thoughts and emotions of the other person makes us more astute in recognizing their meaning, even if it is not spoken.

How does this help us in our job search? We become more sensitive to the needs of others. We also become more sensitive to ourselves. Emotional intelligence includes self-regulation which is a part of mindfulness-being mindful of our own thoughts and feelings. When we are in touch with these things we are better able to face the trials that beset us, the interruptions, the aggravations, and the stress.

Imagine yourself in an interview and the person gets interrupted with a looming crisis. You are listening to what's happening, and understanding the plight of the company at that moment. All of a sudden, it comes to you, a solution you once used when in a similar situation. Very quietly, once alone with the interviewer, you mention this idea. The person looks at you surprised, and then calls the supervisor to tell them to do just what you've recommended. Sound impossible? These things happen when you focus on what others need. You have stepped inside their shoes and suddenly the ideas fly into your mind. Talk about leaving a good impression, the interviewer will not forget you very quickly.

This mindfulness also makes you a go-to person when friends and colleagues need someone with whom they can talk things over. They know they will get sound advice, calmly stated, on target. When you don't mind taking a few minutes, you will reap the benefits ten-fold when they refer you for a job, or a project. You will take your personal brand from sterling to gold, or even platinum.

30. YOUR SPORTING BRAND

Witnessing the Wimbledon finals was impressive last year, first, you have the win by Serena Williams despite enormous odds including fighting serious disease. Second, Roger Federer wins his seventh Wimbledon title making him the number one ranked tennis player at the age of 31. And finally, Andrew Murray comes in second, the native son at Wimbledon, but showing promise and receiving accolades from his countrymen who so desperately hoped that he would win. Murray's speech after the game had to have given even the hardest of hearts a lump in their throats as he fought back tears to get control of his own powerful emotions. It was moving and drew the crowds closer to him than they had ever been.

What can we extrapolate from these events for our personal brand? Serena Williams' brand is one that never gives up despite all odds. Her very name will signify this in the mind of the public. Roger Federer will be perceived as someone who defies age and the odds and who loves the sport through and through. Andrew Murray will become the United Kingdom's new hope, a message no doubt linked to the rejuvenation of many British institutions including the new monarchy.

How can your actions support the message you create with your brand? If you want recognition, are there activities that you can engage in to attain it. Maybe you would like to be nominated as the top professional in your field by a local trade association. You would have to work towards this goal that will yield many intangible benefits. Just as these tennis players have self-discipline and a strong work ethic, you too will have to apply yourself to gaining the nomination. We only see them on the day that they win and make speeches, but we need to examine what goes into that day. Months, years of hard work, sacrifice in order to be the best. Are we willing to make those efforts?

Let's say you would like to be known for charitable works? You would have to select a non-profit group whose mission is something that is important to you. Once you choose the group, you will be giving them your time and efforts, and in time you will receive recognition from your peers. These activities expose you to a completely different segment of the population, enabling you to make new acquaintances and contacts, but the recognition doesn't come overnight. What does tend to happen almost immediately is a sense of well-being that comes from being involved in the plight of others less fortunate, or a cause that is close to our hearts. This kind of activity defines you in a way that regular work activities don't. Your involvement says something about you that you care, that you are willing to make an effort for something larger than yourself. And in that moment, you have defined yourself as that kind of human being, no less skilled at your profession, but perhaps a bit wiser demonstrating what your personal brand is made of.

31.   YOUR TEAM BRAND

There they are: the five young ladies who won the Olympic Gold Medal for gymnastics: Mc Kayla Maroney, Kyla Ross, Alexandra Raisman, Gabrielle Douglas and Jordyn Wieber. What a team! Like every team, their journey is fraught with setbacks, frustrations and ultimately, triumphs.   Early in the week we are witness to the heartbreak of Jordyn Wieber, 2011 World Champion, not making the competition.   Having placed fourth with Aly Raisman and Gabby Douglas placing before her, they were the only two U.S. gymnasts allowed to go on to the finals. The most impressive part is that while devastated, Jordyn remains in the game, focused, supporting her teammates and enabling them overcome the odds. We then see them working together to bring home the gold medal for the first time since 1996.

This team is invincible, despite their personal setbacks; they work together having an unconscious connection to one another, cheering each other on even as they compete against each other. It is truly teamwork at its best. Branding yourself as a team does mean that there is some personal sacrifice. Maybe it means your lows are not so low, and your win, like Gabby Douglas winning the Gold Medal for gymnastics, is also a statement for the team. We heard the story of Gabby giving up home and family to live with strangers far away in order to train with a top coach. It is the team environment that has allowed them to thrive and improve. The team is there for Jordyn just as she is there for them. They absorb the blow of Aly not making bronze due to a scoring method that allows a Russian gymnast who fell off the balance beam, to advance over her in the overall score.

The core of the team brand is that the team stands for something. Each person gives up a little of their autonomy for the good of the team. It doesn't mean that they can't be the unique person they are complete with flaws, but a common thread unites them and moves them forward on their joint goal. Many of them are best friends; the emotions have to be enormous. On one hand you're winning, but your best friend just lost their chance. It's an agonizing moment. They sail through it with ease and selflessness. They never abandon those ties they have to one another. The cult of leadership will tell you that a leader is not a good team member, but I think it is the opposite, for only when you can be a part of that team, participating in the group's collective result, can you be an effective leader of others. You have to internalize that joint fate: we are in this together, we must succeed. And that's an unstoppable team brand. So look around you, to your workgroups, departments and teams or even your company. Are you engaged in your collective outcome? Are you able to take one for the team? Can you connect with your colleagues and share your ups and downs, never failing to be there for them? These attributes are the things that make a team, and give that team its successful brand.

32. BECOMING YOUR OWN BRAND CHAMPION

Recently the writer had the opportunity to visit the sales office of the new Marlins Stadium. Wow, what a beauty! It was all about tying the stadium to Miami (after all it's where the former Orange Bowl stadium was). You can see the skyline in the distance. And it's 'destination' ballpark, meaning you don't just go for a game, you go for an experience: to enjoy baseball and other amenities like shopping, restaurants, a beautiful aquarium behind home plate (after all it's the MARLINS, right?).

I think it will have a revitalizing effect on the area beyond baseball, although winning games and having a ballpark filled with enthusiastic fans is a wonderful thing. Being originally from the land of the Mets and Yankees-it's hard to understand why the park isn't filled. But now we have this new stadium with a roof when needed, and the retractable roof will even cover you on your way out of the stadium, talk about creature comforts.

And I guess that's what is impressive, the comfort, the caring that you will experience in this new arena. Every detail has been attended to. It's like telling the public: 'we're doing it right, we want you to enjoy, bring your friends and family and you're not going to be limited to just watching game, you can hang out too, or shop till you drop'.

Championing a brand is all about that: it's speaking a special language of love for your brand, extending yourself. How else can you make a difference and cut through all the other brand messages? Giving of yourself without measuring, sharing ideas, thoughts, kind words-this is the way to build rapport and recognition of your personal brand. Ensure others are comfortable: how can I make things easier for my fellow employees, customers, coworkers, neighbors? Kindness has to be the greatest brand attribute, there is never enough of it, but if you espouse it, it becomes ingrained in your own brand. You're not only someone people come to for expertise, but because they feel welcomed, comfortable, 'safe'.

Opening yourself up to be able to give these things takes work. You have to gather the perceptions of others around you, so you can test your brand message. What do they say about you? How do they feel about you? Or are you one more headache they have to deal with? Give people their moment in the sun, show your appreciation, give praise and build them up. Be consistent, or people will wonder which part of you they will get on any given day. People who feel good about themselves in your presence will want to see more of you, will be more effective, productive. This in turn will reflect well on your brand. It's a win-win all around.

I may enjoy a few baseball games from time to time, but I'm going to love going to this interesting and dynamic new place which caters to all of my needs, a place where my family and friends want to go too. Now if I can incorporate that into my personal brand-well-I can be my own brand champion too!

33. DISCOVERING YOUR INNER BRAND

At a recent big game day at Marlin's Stadium, they hosted 'Bark at the Park'. 'Bark at the Park' is an event that the Marlins co-sponsor with the humane societies of Miami Dade and Broward. You can bring your dog and sit in a special section of the stadium. This year, in the new stadium, it's an afternoon game. They are ready for the crowds of people with their dogs that arrive with leashes, caps, tee shirts. You can take a picture with your best friend at the entrance, and head up the ramp to the Vista level. No complaints here, although it's the highest level, it has a great view of the field. There are amenities for the dogs such as water bowls at each level of the ascending ramp, a walking area covered with faux grass, and giveaways such as bag clips and water bottles.

Of course there are the obvious comparisons of dogs with masters. The tiny little dog who fits in a purse with a very feminine young women, or the dyed in the wool baseball fan with a miniature bulldog. But there are also those anomalies, like small dogs with very manly looking men, and a waif-like female with an Irish setter. The dogs seemed happy to be included in the fun, there were a few near-conflicts, such as two beagles interacting with a dachshund, but all was settled quickly. Many of the owners took advantage of the day to outfit their pets in team clothing, logos and all. Most sported either a neckerchief or a cap-when they stayed on their heads. The atmosphere in the Vista section was fairly upbeat, and the game did not disappoint. Justin Ruggiano won the game with a single, bringing the score to 5-4 over the San Diego Padres.

If you are a pet owner, there's something special about bringing your pet to an event. Normally you're leaving them home; here they are with you enjoying the moment. It's a chance to define you, who you really are. We are probably ourselves most truly and authentically when we are with our pets. We are that part of us that no one sees. How we behave with our pets and even how we decide to dress them is a reflection of how we perceive the world around us. We are interacting with this dependent creature and celebrating them. When we do this, we are also saying who we are. This activity also engages others.

The people around you acknowledge you, your pet, and your point of view. They are reflecting their own selves with their pets and communicating that to you. It's an exchange that seems to define all of us; we are there to enjoy a game and the presence of this member of the family. It amazes me that on these occasions everyone seems to get along. The crowd seems mellow, subdued yet joyous. Could it be at that moment we've all become part of one big pack, dog and human? If we are expressing our inner nature then I think our nature is a peaceful one. It's a being that just wants to get along and enjoy the triumphs as they come while sharing in the setbacks. I encourage you to allow your inner domestic animal define you; you might just discover your most genuine personal brand.

34. TAKING THE HEAT FOR YOUR PERSONAL BRAND

As Miami prepares to celebrate the second victorious win of the fabulous Heat, we think about how this winning brand came about. A few years ago LeBron James made the decision to join the Miami Heat in order to play with 2003 draft class pals Dwayne Wade and Chris Bosch. The Cleveland Cavaliers were not only sad, but downright angry about LeBron's leaving them for Miami, but he wanted to win a championship and felt that it was his chance. Of course announcing the move in the way he did not ingratiate him to the press and fans despite having telecast his choice to earn money for a children's charity. The second year he made good on his promise and they won the NBA Championship. Now in 2013, they have gone on to win it again.

LeBron James was able to put his heart and his talent into this new environment and not only did it work for him, but it's become a defining moment. If we're lucky and smart and work real hard we might get a chance to achieve that dream. What makes us that person, the unmistakable, imperceptible nuance can be just that, those decisions at a turning point in our careers or our lives that turns the tide in our direction and enables us to become the person we've dreamed of being.

What moment is that for you? Where do you stand in the middle of the crossroads of your own career? Is it a defining moment that you choose to join a new company, or perhaps you head out on your own into an entrepreneurial venture? What does that choice say about you and your brand? For most of us, it may seem at the time that our lives are crowded speedways with lots of intersections that can take us in different directions.

How do we go about finding the right road to take, the one that will not only define us, but enable us to demonstrate who we really are and what we are really made of? It starts with knowing what is right for you within. If we are inwardly one thing and portray a mask to the world, at one point or another, the true image will emerge. It is that truth which distinguishes your brand. Following your passion takes courage. Being who you are, integral, inside and out, takes honesty and requires us to expose ourselves to scrutiny whether our own, or that of others. In the final analysis, it is how we embody our personal brand.

35. DEFINING YOUR INTERIOR BRAND

What's important? Your personal brand is very important. Yes, that's what we write about and your brand should reflect your identity. But is it more important than wars being fought, or terrorists plotting attacks on the US, or air collisions and collapsing buildings? Well it's different. Somehow it's the issue that hit home this past week for many people. Jason Collins, NBA star of the Boston Celtics admitted openly that he was gay. For sports, for basketball, this was a big step. Many have called him a hero. Now there is no denying that this man has suffered by keeping the secret of his true identity, and it was a relief for him to open up about it. He had endured 'years of misery' and not even his brother was aware. That has got to be a burden for someone to carry around.

A personal brand is something you are trying to communicate to others about yourself. It is meant to define you. We have certainly tried to give suggestions on getting to that authentic self and letting it be known to the world, whether through an elevator pitch, or some soul searching, or the choice of approach in interviewing and resume writing. But having to reveal your innermost secret to the world publicly is definitely a bold step in defining your personal brand.

Jason Collins expended energy in guarding his secret just as we have encouraged people to try to reveal what is unique about them when searching for a job or a career. He had to do the opposite, keep his true inner being from everyone. This creates tremendous isolation and even alienation. This isolation keeps us from truly engaging with others we meet during the course of business. If we cannot be our true selves, there is something inauthentic about all of our dealings. On this personal level this revelation is a breakthrough for Jason Collins. He realized that his world did not fall apart, although it is irrevocably changed. This change will bring about a different level of engagement in his sports career and in his personal life.

Collins is being called a hero for coming forward with this information, but really all he has done is to square with us about who he really is. For those of us looking to make a contribution, we should try to be true to ourselves right from the start. Our sports icons represent a strong focus of our society, some might say too strong, for as much as I am glad that Jason Collins is being honest with himself and the world, I can only hope that we continue to rally around the service men and women who are out there defending us, and the first responders when crisis hits, who are truly the heroes we must emulate in our own personal brand.

36. EXPLAINING YOUR BRAND MESSAGE

The morning after the recent presidential election, things seemed somewhat still the same. There was a storm raging in the Northeast; the stock market took a plunge. We will probably spend the next six months thinking, "Would this have happened if Romney had been elected president?" Well, it's hard to say isn't it? We don't know what's ahead. We don't know if the Congress will work across party lines to get the United States out of the economic troubles we're in. We have no sense of trust that our elected officials will take our concerns to heart and do something about it.

So what do we know? Well, we know that Barack Obama won a second term in office despite a bad economy high unemployment and massive discontent. We know that the Republican Party is left scratching their heads thinking that the race was about the economy, but at the end, maybe it wasn't. So we must consider what was happening and how is that connected to our own personal brand. First of all, a brand has to stand for something, it has to be good at solving some problem, and it needs the unique selling proposition. A brand needs something at its core that is unique and is not a feature of any other brand. With an individual, you would think that this is easy; after all, don't we all have an individual DNA code? Yes, at the molecular level, but here we are talking about something that sets us apart in the minds of the public. Maybe it's that thousand watt smile we always seem to have, or a signature saying that we often repeat. I recall a colleague who was fond of 'that being said', which in many cases is redundant since what it is has already been said! I would count the number of times he used that phrase during management meetings. At least it kept me awake!

Mitt Romney is an accomplished man with many facets. He ran the Olympics; he is the former governor of Massachusetts, and the former CEO of Bain and Company, a well-respected consulting firm. He is well spoken, makes a great appearance. So what is it that we didn't like, couldn't relate to, or didn't trust about him? Political pundits say he started the race as a moderate, became more conservative and then migrated back towards the center at the end. Could it be confusion over just what he does represent? YES! A unique selling proposition has to be simple and clear. We don't have time to figure it out, we need to decide can I trust this guy or not?

I think as a moderate, Mr. Romney was appealing, but when he became more conservative it did not seem real. At the end, he left us confused as to what he stood for. Although we need a leader who can change and evolve, we must first be convinced we can trust his judgment no matter what. The clarity of the message was not compelling. Of course some of the sound bite comments didn't help. Why were these comments disconcerting? If we don't completely trust a person, and then hear them use terms to describe people as percentages or binders, it smacks of objectification: we are all just numbers to him. That certainly doesn't make his personal brand an approachable one.

It came down to electing someone whose message you understood, whose actions were congruent with that message. It makes it easier for us to relate to someone, when they are more or less the same person every day. We know where they are coming from, we don't always approve or agree, but at least we have an idea of what we're in for. Herein our lesson: a personal brand has to be tried and true, it must represent those basic beliefs through our actions every day. If we cannot convey that clearly into the minds of our public, then we risk losing them. Keep the message clear and simple, be true to that message over time, you're a lot easier to believe when you are living your personal brand.

Marylou P. Kay

37. HOW DOES STYLE DIFFERENCE AFFECT A BRAND?

We've talked about branding defining your place in the world, and backing up that brand, but the writer was watching some 'Full Frontal Fashion' programs highlighting two fashion icons, Karl Lagerfeld, who designs for Fendi, and Jean Paul Gaultier preparing for their fashion shows. Both geniuses, they are very different one from another.

Karl Lagerfeld is cool, calm, collected. He claims he does not have emotions. When he looked at the clothing the staff had made from his designs, he made short comments 'this works', 'this needs help'. He didn't ridicule anyone or belabor the issue, but his direction was received and acted upon immediately. During interviews, Maria, who has been with Karl over 20 years, said 'I love Karl, we understand each other'. The first time Maria made one of Karl's designs, he exclaimed 'Finally someone who understands what I design'.

In contrast, Jean Paul Gaultier is everywhere at once, making comments, jubilant, upset, laughing and anguished within the space of a few minutes. His team is equally enamored of him, working furiously long hours trying to finish clothing for the big fashion show. Gaultier makes last minute changes, shortens one dress, takes the sleeves off another and put long gloves on to cover the model's arms, but everyone there including the models is extremely motivated, and they run to take care of every last detail.

The restraint and severity of Karl Lagerfeld's fashions belie his controlled personality. The ebullience and expressiveness of Gaultier's creations reflect well his fervid countenance. So how does your personal style define you and your brand?

Does your manner and your speech convey the personal brand message you want to send? They say 'clothes makes the man'. Does your mode of dress reflect what you are trying to project? Sound advice suggests that you dress for the role you would like to play. Think about what impression you want to leave with people, this is especially important during an interview, or when making a presentation. Dissonance occurs when these two are not linked, for example you go to an interview in shorts and flip flops. The impression will be that you don't want the job-unless you're interviewing to be a lifeguard!

Do you pay attention to how you speak to people? In order to communicate your personal 'brand value' you need to look them in the eye, speak clearly, and answer any questions graciously, without impatience. This mode of address demonstrates that you are serious, self-composed. It doesn't mean you can't make a joke, but it does mean you are reflecting the importance you attribute to this interaction. And taking phone calls or texts is rude! Make no mistake about that. Taking a call means you don't value the person who is in front of you-with certain exceptions in emergencies, of course.
So get out there and project that amazing person that you are, interactive, dynamic, and personable, because that will define your personal brand almost more than anything else can.

IV HOLIDAYS AND BRANDING

38. REINVENTING YOUR BRAND

So here we are at the end run of the holiday season, with our New Year's resolutions and our best intentions. We have some trepidation, and so we welcome the year a little more warmly hoping to overcome any negative vibes that seem to pervade the air around us.

As we prepare ourselves for the realities of the New Year, many of us are in job search mode, some due to corporate layoffs, and others due to the fact that there are more opportunities available. And there is plenty of good career and job search advice out there. Since we dwell more than a little on personal branding topics here, it's worth our time to talk a little about that brand building tool: LinkedIn. I am a fervent LinkedIn member. I find it extremely useful to connect with people I haven't seen in some time, or to make new connections. There are so many things you can do: join groups with similar interests, or even start your own group. You can read about current events and developments and indicate your agreement or disagreement with a host of topics. You can answer questions and be perceived as an expert, you can pose questions and poll colleagues about issues that concern you.

The idea about networking is that you are sharing your expertise, knowledge, contacts with others, and they are reciprocating. We all know this is not always the case. So a recent article entitled "Why a request to connect gets ignored on LinkedIn" is a great refresher on the basics of networking. J.T. O'Donnell quotes some of the requests she's gotten including one from someone she didn't know asking for career support pro bono after the individual spent a lot of money on career services that did not yield any results. It's hard to believe that someone would think that their personal circumstance is compelling enough to garner a total stranger to step in and solve the problem for you while not even considering how they could reciprocate with any services or contacts. It's absurd, and yet they clearly don't understand why they can't get an interview, much less a job.

That approach is all about taking. It is not done in the true spirit of networking which is: friendly interaction for mutual benefit. It's about give and take, not just getting something for free without giving something in return. The person you approach has to see what might be in it for them. If you do not think of what benefit there could be for the other person, you will never master the art of networking.

How many times have I received a request to connect from someone I don't know, with whom I have nothing in common, and who has not even taken a couple of minutes to explain why they would like to connect with me. I'm not expecting a long letter; I just want to make some sense of the request.

Another way to connect with people is an interesting technique called 'cluster networking' where you connect with different groups of colleagues and contacts in a way that will feel more natural. After all, who doesn't want to connect with former colleagues, it's great to catch up and sometimes reform the relationship in the present time. Make sure your networking brand is a giving brand, a reciprocal brand. Share your expertise and you will be surprised at the results. It's only fair and it gives you a more meaningful personal brand.

Marylou P. Kay

39. LABOR DAY AND YOUR BRAND

It's that time of year again, the kids are back at school, the universities are reopened and we celebrate that last hallmark of summer fun: Labor Day Weekend. This year with Democrats and Republicans fighting it out in negative advertising each trying to attack the other's brand, it's a bittersweet celebration. After all, how do you celebrate Labor Day when so many people are not working? It's not for lack of trying; twenty two million Americans cannot find a job. Taxes and mortgages are not being paid. Foreclosures continue and family members who barely speak are now moving in with each other to save money. Many states are being pushed to the limit, pulling funds designated for community improvements just to keep the unemployment claims paid.

Labor Day evokes the times when there were parades, when people were proud of their labors because they had a good job that was going to last them a long time. They were not ashamed of manual labor in those days, before manual labor was relegated to illegal aliens. Now in 2012 union membership is down to seven percent of the population, it is an all-time low. As much as unions try to make a comeback, the lack of real power over job retention does not really support their cause. If they make a fuss, the company closes the factory and relocates the jobs elsewhere. Working with unions, one of the things that amazes me is how employees think a union is going to help them if a company goes out of business.

So we have the AFL-CIO working on getting people to vote in the upcoming elections. They are becoming civic activists trying to further their cause through the general elections, hoping to have a President who supports them. And this administration has supported them, yet somehow they cannot seem to get the new legislation passed. Labor Day Weekend, so many people wish they were laboring and bringing home a paycheck. It doesn't work that way. Companies are afraid of the future and so they do not build up their employee base for fear they may have to lay them off ultimately. For the AFL-CIO it is a smart move, a re-branding effort. With so few labor battles to be fought, they have come up with a new way to keep mention of them top most in the minds of the working public by encouraging people to vote. It's a kinder, gentler way to stay in the game.

We can take this lesson to our personal brand. For what activity have we been known which since then has morphed into something lackluster? How do we go about brushing the dust off that personal brand? By staying involved in what's going on around us and looking for ways we can take our existing skillset and transition it to an area needing new talent and ideals. Use your existing strengths in new arenas. It does take some self-assessment, some courage to look at yourself and figure out what you could do that you enjoy, but it will be worth the effort when you find yourself aligned with something bold, exciting that brands you in a whole new light.

40. WHAT DEFINES YOUR THANKSGIVING BRAND?

Here we are, the eve of the most celebrated holiday in the United States. It's non-denominational and centers on being thankful as some of the first arrivals to our shores hundreds of years ago. Not to belabor the point about how Native Americans feel about this, they may not be so thankful after all.

No, what I want to talk about is how are you defining your personal brand on Thanksgiving? For in the last week we have been bombarded with "Black Friday" advertisements (just when we thought it was safe to put the TV on after the elections) pitching to us the need to start Holiday shopping during the day of Thanksgiving. Some say it started when we allowed stores to be open on Sundays, others talk about some fifteen or twenty years ago when the preponderance of a free day after Thanksgiving gave people the impetus to start on their shopping lists in advance. However it has come about, the time has come creeping up on the actual holiday itself. First it was getting to the store at 6 am on Friday. Then it progressed to 12 midnight, and lo and behold, we now have major retailers opening their doors on Thanksgiving day for those big sales and door busters.

What does this mean about us? Well, we're trying to save money. We're hoping to jumpstart the economy. All that is understandable. We are also taking away our family time. The simple pleasure of cherishing our relationships, savoring those good foods, and being grateful for the abundance in our lives is thrown by the wayside.

Somehow if consumerism is all that defines us it seems sad. Maybe you just wanted time to have a snooze after a dinner, or watch the football game, or catch up with Uncle Harry and Aunt Nellie. Now you have to have a plan of how to consume your meal and then start your attack on the local mall.

Of course the employees of these establishments are up in arms. Many of them are protesting, why they should have to give up their holiday for their jobs. And these days good jobs are scarce. Of course, there have always been pharmacies open, doctors on call, fire, police, so this is not new for many people. Now however, it's becoming much more common for people to have to give up their holiday.

When I think of the Americans serving in the armed forces, eating at some base somewhere and longing for home, I just don't think what they're missing is a run to the mall with hordes of people pushing and shouting. When I imagine those people who no longer have homes after Hurricane Sandy, I cannot conceive of them waiting in long lines to get the first access to consumer goods. Even if there were some item I desperately needed, I wouldn't want that activity to define my Thanksgiving. Nobler minds than mine have tackled this question, even before there was a holiday:

> To everything there is a season, and a time to every purpose under the heaven: a time to be born, and a time to die; a time to plant, and a time to pluck up that which is planted; A time to kill, and a Time to heal; a time to break down, and a time to build up;
> I know that there is no good in them, but for a man to rejoice, and to do good in his life. And also that every man should eat and drink, and enjoy the good of all his labor, it is the gift of God. I know that, whatsoever God

doeth, it shall be forever: nothing can be put to it, or anything taken from it: and God doeth it, that men should fear before him. (Ecclesiastes 3, King James Version)

You understand my meaning. Here we have this beautiful world we've been given, yes, fraught with difficulties and wars. And on the day we set aside to be thankful, we abandon to pursue a discounted flat screen television.

We've often spoken about being true to your personal brand, and letting it stand for something. So on the eve of this very American Holiday, I'm asking you to consider: what defines your personal brand at Thanksgiving? Is it to shop early and get the bargains? Or is it a time to reflect and enjoy with loved ones while you ponder your good fortune. Even if we are not so fortunate, we can have something to be grateful for be it the breath we are taking. Happy Thanksgiving!

Marylou P. Kay

41. HOLIDAY NETWORKING AND YOUR BRAND

Well, here it is that time of year when we set to merrymaking in the extreme. And it's all allowed! We can overeat and drink and think nothing of it until January 2nd when we'll be weighing in at the gym. So what about your personal brand? Are you the one with the lampshade on your head at the office holiday party? Or do you skip it altogether explaining you have a big project to finish for the boss?

Well, most of us seem to enjoy gatherings in whatever setting. Companies here in Miami give parties at restaurants, in the workplace, and even in their homes. Every group-from work, to non-profit, to church choirs, to social groups, or bowling leagues has some kind of holiday party. At the risk of rehashing things you might already know, I'm going to discuss it from your personal brand's perspective.

Office holiday gathering: you want to brand yourself as participative, collaborative, but not overly boisterous. So dress appropriately, smile and try to make the rounds to chat with colleagues and bosses. This is not the time to get wasted on the punch. It is the time to demonstrate your excellent interpersonal skills and your ability to talk about interesting things that have nothing to do with business.

Non-profit: this might be an opportunity to show off your organization skills. Offer to help out with the guest list, or escorting people around, it demonstrates your flexibility. If it's a 'Gala' make sure you pull out your best duds-tuxedo, ball gown, etc. These are often 'dress to impress' events.

Church groups: make your special recipe, whatever it is and go along for some laughs. It doesn't hurt to exhibit your light side. Attire is probably casual, holiday-themed depending on the group.
Bowling league: this is another place to show you're in the mix-helping to organize a special holiday-themed game or contest.
Social group/professional group: similar to the office party you don't want to get crazy, but do join in the conga line, line dance, or whatever other relatively innocuous activity they have going on.

Result: you will be perceived as someone who joins in, a 'regular' guy/gal. Here you want to look pulled together or 'smart', but avoid anything too outrageous or revealing, unless you want everyone to remember you that way(that's a personal brand statement too!).
Unless you are a hermit, (which by the very nature of our southeast Florida area is impossible), you will be bombarded with invitations and places to let loose. There is nothing wrong with any of this-it gives you an opportunity once again to demonstrate your personal brand: someone who participates, makes jokes, cultivates new contacts, organizes, and knows how to behave appropriately in any setting. The perfect guest. Is there anything wrong with that? Hey, it's a break from the masses at the mall, AND you just might end up enjoying yourself! Jingle Jingle.

42. CREATING A PERSONAL HOLIDAY BRAND

The frenetic holiday season is upon us. It gets dark early and all these cars are rushing somewhere, maybe to buy gifts or special food items to prepare for family and friends. It starts just after Thanksgiving, or right on it actually this year, and continues until early January. I think of January 6th as the end marker since it's the Christian Epiphany when supposedly the Three Wise Kings or Magi arrive in Bethlehem. This last one is an interesting one that we don't much celebrate in the U.S. but in France it's called the 'Fête des Rois', and you eat a special cake that has a bean or token baked in it. The person who gets the token is given a crown-King for a day.

Whether you celebrate Christmas, Chanukah, Kwanzaa, or the 'Fête des Rois', this is a festive time of year. Parties, casual and formal, abound offering opportunities to network, catch up, or even conduct new business. Festive attire is a part of the setting, and foods, drinks and gifts all play a part in the merrymaking. No matter what you do to celebrate, you have to go out and find the gifts, attire, food, then attend the events. You are required to be out and about.

Being from the northeast originally, I always thought of this time of year as a challenge. It's dark, it's cold, there's usually some kind of weather issue endangering mobility. This is what led me to come up with my holiday theory, which I will share with you here. I believe that many more of us have Seasonal Affective Disorder (S.A.D.) than is recognized. So this holiday time of year with lights and gaiety is meant to shake off those doldrums and get us out and about. If you're visiting brightly lit stores or Holiday displays, you're less likely to feel the effects of this mood disorder, also known as winter depression, winter blues, or seasonal depression. It occurs in up to 10 percent of the population, and is more aggravated in northern climes. Northern Finland and Alaska are some of the places with the highest percentages. Some estimates put it much higher at 35% but many of the cases are milder versions.

S.A.D. is a disorder in which people who have normal mental health throughout most of the year experience depressive symptoms in the winter or autumn year after year. My theory is that these Holiday events force us to get the light and exposure that we are missing. People with S.A.D. often receive light therapy with sunlight or bright lights, antidepressant medication, ionized-air administration and melatonin supplements. So what propels you to pursue the festive activities? Is it to chase away those winter blues, or are you out there to acquire some new business?

Living in Florida, we seem to get more light and the problem isn't as severe as up north, something that makes me very happy for affected as I was with S.A.D., I went about the Holiday season with grim determination and dread, no doubt due to light deprivation and a little stress. It always seemed to be one of the busiest times at work, with the most parties and all that darkness. Nowadays, I can enjoy the season a little more, choose my festivities wisely and not feel as burdened as before. So for you my readers, I wish you all the light possible during this season and hope you will make an effort to get out and network your personal holiday brand in a way that suits you and your authentic 'inner' brand.

43. BRANDING THE HOLIDAYS YOUR WAY

The holidays are almost over. Things are calming down, presents opened, meals cooked and consumed, and you sit back and put your feet up and reflect on what's been going on for the past two months leading up to the holidays. You think about these holidays and ones gone by, the people you've loved and lost and those who are still with you. How has that love been demonstrated?

And then you contemplate how have I left my mark on the holiday? Have I been able to express how I felt about those that I have in my life? Have I shown kindness? Have I dedicated myself to meaningful activities?

It's important to celebrate in your personal style, do the things that make you and others happy and resist getting caught up in hype and consumerism. It's your life after all and your brand, you have to make sure it stands for something and reflects who you really are. Normally in this column we address your personal brand in relation to the world of business and career. Here we are asking you to take a closer look at other parts of your life and make sure you are living a life that is authentically you.

That may mean you let people know that it's low-key this year, you're scaling back or not exchanging gifts at all. It may mean you try to resurrect some favorite recipe from your childhood and recreate some memories. Or that you choose to meet with friends you normally don't see. Maybe you opt for spending some time alone, doing something very personal yet meaningful. Your brand means you define just what it is that makes it a holiday for you. You may get some pushback from those around you who don't appreciate the change of approach. And you might just start a new tradition that reflects your personal brand.

V THE DARK SIDE

144. CAN YOU HURT YOUR PERSONAL BRAND?

Recent events tell us that there are some things that can hurt your personal brand. When Lebron James announced he was going to the Miami Heat, he made a personal choice, one that resonated with him: he joined fellow teammates he had played with in the Olympics. This was something very important to him, more than money, or than having the glory for himself. One might say he is the classic 'millennial' he wants to be with his friends, and that balance means more to him than anything else, except maybe his family, but they were supportive of this move. So he has not hurt his brand, but he will now be defined by that choice to be a part of a team, or a select group on a team.

Now balance, on the other hand, is not what Mel Gibson has these days. Forget the heartthrob, eager young actor of 'Gallipoli', 'Mrs. Soffel', 'The year of Living Dangerously' , or the director/producer of 'Braveheart' and 'The Passion of the Christ.' No, now he's a rich, middle-aged man with some very un-PC ideas that he seems to share quite openly, or in hostile aggressive ways. One title for him this morning was 'Mad Mel' parodying one of his earlier Aussie movies, 'Mad Max' -a man driven over the edge by grief at losing his wife to a futuristic gang.

In Mel's current troubles, his wife (very much alive) is still the cause of his distress, but it's of that typical nasty, bitter, matrimonial kind. And the personal brand of Mel Gibson becomes 'Mad Mel' -a kind of deranged, out of control Wildman-maybe he's going for a remake of 'The Werewolf.'

45. YOUR BRAND: GONE IN 60 SECONDS

You do all the right things, you train, you get an education, you compete in sports, you serve in the military, you're a duty-conscious royal, or maybe you run for public office. Making it big in this world of ours takes tenacity, effort, ambition, drive. You want to show the world what you're made of, maybe you want to do good things, or stand for something important. You want to build your personal brand. And then, in one story, one remark, one minute that you weren't watching, it goes south on you. You find that they are paying attention to you for all the wrong reasons. Years of hard work go down the drain. Education, career, medals, trophies, years of public service come to nothing when you make a thoughtless comment, you give up the good fight against those who would damage your reputation, or you show up in an immodest photo, as in the recent cases of our three subjects.

Republican Senate candidate Todd Akin of Missouri said that victims of "legitimate" rape can't get pregnant because "the female body has ways to try to shut that whole thing down." It's an unthinkable comment that demonstrates lack of scientific knowledge as well as disrespect for women. The Republican Party has asked him to step out of his race, yet Akin insists on staying in. How does he think he will be able to lead when we associate his brand with stupidity and callous disregard? Mr. Akin no doubt has done his best to rise in politics. His comment about rape and pregnancy is indefensible and when questioned, he really offers no explanation to justify it. He parrots his supposed family values platform, but of course, women are usually a part of a family.

The case of Lance Armstrong is particularly disturbing. Armstrong won the Tour de France seven times. He fought cancer and won. He has never tested positive for doping, yet he will be stripped of all his medals by the USADA because he is tired of fighting their claims. A federal judge wrote last week, "USADA's conduct raises serious questions about whether its real interest in charging Armstrong is to combat doping, or if it is acting according to less noble motives." They have pursued him for a very long time. Lance Armstrong is a man with a strong personal brand who commands our respect. He is a cycling legend who will now be banned from the sport. One judgment from an agency that seems to have a hidden agenda has robbed him of that sterling brand.

And finally, Prince Harry, royal bad boy, has none of the pathos of Mr. Armstrong, or the hypocrisy of Mr. Akin, but shows how fragile a personal brand can be nonetheless. We thrill to Harry's exploits, whether on a good will tour for the Queen, or on his military training missions. We know he's fun loving, and sometimes a bit naughty, but his recent indecorous act leaves us disillusioned.

After the thrill of the London Olympics and the pomp of his grandmother's Golden Jubilee, I'm sure the British public is more than disappointed, although perhaps not surprised. The sad part here is Harry's personal brand, it is now officially tarnished. All the very good things he's been doing diplomatically and in the military now fade a bit leaving us disconcerted about what kind of mark he is trying to leave.

The lesson for us about a personal brand is that it's many years in the building, but quickly sullied. Once tainted, can we rehabilitate a personal brand? We have seen numerous incidents of reinvigorated personal brands of people who come back into the limelight even stronger. You can survive in the face of public fury. Reconstructing your brand may start with the basics: being true to your purpose, clarifying your message, and actions that support your personal brand.

Marylou P. Kay

46. NEWTOWN: A TRAGIC BRAND

We've discussed in the past how your brand is your bond, you have to back it up with actions. The tragedy we have witnessed this past week is something that is unfathomable. How does this happen? The very woman who thinking she would give her son a skill by teaching him to shoot a gun, is murdered by that well developed precision. Worse, he goes to the local school and shoots 20 innocent children who still had their baby teeth. These children were born in 2005, not a very long time ago. And their lives are cut short because of the poor judgment of a mother, a community.

Wherever you stand on guns and mental illness, you know that the combination of the two is lethal. I can understand those who have a gun to protect themselves and their families or to go hunting; but where does that warrant an assault rifle. There is only one result to be obtained with such a weapon: killing in rapid succession. If the person were in a war zone it could possibly be justified, but suburban Connecticut? And if you're going to collect guns, then have them locked in a display case, not accessible. We have a violent country and it's a violent world, but when did the love of playing shooting games turn into an unfeeling insensitivity to the pain of others?

Here we are about to celebrate the birth of Christ, a pacifist, and we are confronted with the violence we have created, almost worshipped in our midst. We make the criminal a hero; they get their fifteen minutes of fame. Why do we want to know all about their lives? The end result is the same, a selfish act of an unfeeling person that has changed the lives of hundreds of people who will never be the same again. I went to an outdoor shopping mall briefly over the weekend.

The sun was setting, the sky aglow with pinks and purples. There were many people shopping, walking with packages, waiting on line to have dinner at a restaurant. Families, couples, young children enveloped in that special twilight hour rush with birds chirping all around. It seemed magical, almost surreal that things could be normal, and then I thought of those families in Connecticut that would celebrate a holiday without a child and a feeling of sadness washed over me. I can't imagine how that might feel.

Tomorrow is the end of the world many say. According to the Mayan calendar, the world must end and restart again. People are waiting in bunkers and 'safe' places with food and necessities ready for the cataclysm that awaits us. If it is indeed the end, perhaps Newtown would become a precursor to the finish line. If we have brought ourselves to this, I'm a little ashamed. I would have wanted it to end with something glorious and beautiful. It is somehow in our human nature to move towards destruction, a kind of psychic entropy that is unavoidable.

Too much of a good thing is the saying. We must have everything in moderation, good and bad. Perhaps the world ending is a way to get the balance back, to reset the natural order of things. We will have to see, won't we?

47. HOW FAR DOES A NEGATIVE BRAND GO?

We've discussed in the past how your brand is your bond, you have to back it up with actions. Yet how does it happen that people with negative brands get to keep on going on doing bad things to people? Darth Vader is one of the most successful negative brands out there, as is Hitler, and of course Osama Bin Laden whose year anniversary of his death was this past week. And the legacy goes on.

Take the story of a friend of mine. She started consulting for a startup bio-tech company with lots of promise; 'we're going to make these products that all farmers will need around the world' they told her. 'We're so energy efficient we're giving back to the grid' they said. 'Using natural biomass, we'll feed the world'. Well, that's impressive, how could you lose? And so my friend helped them out in every way possible, giving structure and reports, even helping them design their business cards as they went public in order to get more money to develop the firm.

Enter right: the investor, a money-man of great wealth giving funds to the firm to develop, but also making lots of money on the sales of the stocks which he bought at a very low price. Enter left, the four inventors of this marvelous technology who claim that the process is a good one, is patented and ready to have plants built to carry out the noble task of feeding the world. Trouble is, they can't explain it, claiming it's too sensitive, or too technical, or some other feasible story for the non-initiate. And when this happens at a very public biotechnology conference, it starts to seem like something is amiss.

So the money man starts wondering about his investment (it's natural) and complains of the high salaries being paid when there is no product being manufactured yet. But the kicker comes when the four inventors resist getting a world class engineering firm to certify that the process works, and worse: that they want a payout of about $7 million for their 'technology'.

My friend, eager to overcome all odds, is struggling with unpaid employees, benefits plans that are not in place and a little thing like Directors and Officers insurance which would protect any officers of the firm from lawsuits in the course of business. Why do you need this you ask? Come on, it's America, we all know what that's about: protect, protect, protect.

As the firm is imploding and my friend is tearfully packing her desk with her lonely cactus plant, she asks 'how could they do this?' and of course the one answer is greed, that good old American value. Talk about a brand! Gordon Gecko here we come, greed never sleeps. There's money to be made even if families are destroyed, employees have no paychecks or benefits, they default on their loans. But those good ol' boys got their money, at the shareholder's expense.

Your negative brand speaks volumes, but at the end of the day, besides the wealth and knowing you pulled something over on the 'suckers' , what do you get out of it? Are their lives any more satisfied? Does it help if you know the money man is dying from an incurable disease? Or the CEO has to go back to being a professor, or one of the inventors has a wife who will divorce him if he can't give her lots of money and a lavish lifestyle on a professor's salary?

That's when a negative brand takes on an all too human face, like Hitler in the bunker, or Osama with porn tapes in his hideout: they are only just people, flawed like you or me, with one glaring difference: we believe in our personal brand that is our word, our bond, our reckoning with the world, our God, ourselves.

48. DEMYSTIFYING A NEGATIVE BRAND

We've all seen the news and heard bit by bit the account of the capture of Osama Bin Laden, head of Al Qaida and world renowned anti American terrorist. Surely one image that will be reflective of our current college age, twenty-something generation is the picture of groups of young people chanting "USA...USA ....USA..." It is quite a change from college revolutions and demonstrations of decades ago. And why? Bin Laden was the arch-enemy, the evil wrongdoer from the Dark Side, a new Hitler. This generation has lived with this bad guy all of their conscious existence. They have always felt that fear, just as a Jewish person growing up in Germany in the 1930's would fear the Third Reich, the Gestapo.

And it wasn't just here in the U.S.; young people around the world have had to live with additional screening in airports, subway bombing plots in Madrid and London, or hotel bombings like Mumbai. The world is a different place to travel in these days, gone are the times of fearing a rip off at a youth hostel, innocent people are losing their lives all the time. Almost like a collective unconscious release of pent up fear, the cheering and chanting erupted at campuses, in cities, at sporting events. Ding Dong the witch is dead!

As we've watched every new report with more details as to how Bin Laden was living in the villa/headquarters in Abbottabad, we are amazed to see he was running Al Qaida, not just a figurehead;, that he had all the necessary technology and was not just sitting over a campfire in a cave. Sure, it's not quite the Ritz or even a Holiday Inn, but there was a real bed and furniture. But perhaps the most surprising and meaningful discovery came early this morning in the form of a video, evidently a candid un-staged one of Bin Laden handled in an old blanket, sitting on the floor, watching television videos of himself, with an old cap and a very gray/white beard. He made a stark contrast to the familiar figure we had come to see in the Al Jazeera videos: gowned and turbaned, with a dark, trimmed beard looking straight into the camera and quietly letting the audience know that he would be planning a new attack, to be on alert. Like the previews of a bad action movie, it was chilling with a sense of unreality about it.

After all, how could one man be doing this to us, the United States, the land of the free, the home of the brave?! The form now huddled before us with his face turned is at the same time horrifying and pathetic. He could be someone's grandfather (he's only 53!), and he's watching himself reveling in his more than ten minutes of fame. Vanity? For someone who had been living in a cave, it's unthinkable.

But then, it wasn't always so, Bin Laden was born to wealth, espoused this nomadic terrorist lifestyle to carry out his life's work. He had to have been aware that at some point he would be caught. He's pathetic, just as beholden to the trappings of Western society with its over glamorization of public figures as any of us might be. So, let there be the shouts and celebrations, but at the end of it is a withered man who chose to hate, who chose destruction and died the way he had lived: violently. He was at the end just as weak and vulnerable as any of us might be, no more a monster, just a self-deluded, flawed human being caught in his own web of violence.

Marylou P. Kay

49. CULTURE OF REVERENCE FOR BAD BEHAVIOR

Do we hold leaders and celebrities in too high esteem to speak out about bad behavior? It would seem so, or we'd be marching on Washington, or Penn State, or Steubenville, Ohio. Such places have witnessed recent actions that are repulsive, morally wrong or illegal. Yet we blithely let it slide by, thinking the 'perpetrator' is now in jail. But shouldn't we examine a culture that permits such actions to occur over time? What exactly is the brand represented by such acts? What kind of a culture allows a person to cause abuse and shame over years of time going largely unnoticed and unsuspected? What kind of a culture can take pleasure in sexually assaulting a woman who is unconscious, and not even a passerby takes action? Have we lost our ability to feel, to empathize with another's pain? Finally, what about a government so politically divided and consumed with ambition that it will hurt the majority of American citizens before settling on a bipartisan compromise? It is not a brand I want to stand behind.

In the U.S. today, we have a culture that puts celebrities on a pedestal as some kind of idol, a false one. Someone has a reality show that makes a lot of money, so we should listen to them, their ideas, their philosophies which produce nothing but revenue for themselves. Do these endless shows contribute to society in any meaningful way? What do we get out of the culture of celebrity? We get nothing, really except a lot of bad behavior that we choose not to emulate. We do not revere anyone for their good actions, for the gift they give to society just by being who they are. We have so few people in that category. While we condemn terrorists for demeaning the value of human life, how different is it from a group of young men attacking an unconscious woman? When we talk about respecting life, how about the lives of the young men victimized by a football coach?

The brand portrayed in the U.S. media is self-serving, money-oriented. If I were to watch these shows and describe the brand, it would not be one that I could relate to, or believe in. The lessons to be learned in respect to our own personal brand are to ask ourselves some tough questions. What do I stand for? Is that clearly articulated as a part of my brand? More and more, we need to more precisely define who we are by the actions we take. We may need some tough minded thinking to better define ourselves and our brand, to make sure it's something we can believe in. More importantly, our brand should represent a standard of behavior that we commit to.

50. AMERICA'S BRAND: TIME TO EXAMINE VALUES

When Greg Smith left Goldman Sachs in March, he did it in a very public way by penning an article in the OP Ed section of the New York Times blasting the Goldman culture. At the end of the article, he resigned. He claimed the culture was now "as toxic and destructive as I've ever seen it." Smith has written a book, "Why I left Goldman Sachs" detailing in depth his twelve year career from the time he graduated college and joined the firm.

Now Goldman Sachs has released the results of an investigation and they have claimed that Smith was a disgruntled employee who was actually being considered for separation from the firm not having lived up to his earlier promise. Does that negate the point about the mean spirited culture at the firm? No, absolutely not.

Goldman Sachs is in business to make money, much of the time profiting by the losses of their customers. Their brand is profits, at any cost. Their customers are no doubt aware of the risk they take;

however it seems surprising that they are willing to continue taking them after this kind of information gets out. Perhaps that's the hardest part to swallow; they are successful because they don't put the interests of their clients first, and that seems to be alright. It is 2012, post-Wall Street crisis, TARP bailout, and Main Street disenchanted with Wall Street, and somehow we don't react to what Mr. Smith is trying to tell us.

Is it because the integrity that we once saw in the large investment houses has gone away, like yesterday's hot stock tip? We have accepted the fact that profits have to come first, that jobs have to be outsourced, that Medicare will have to have vouchers. We go on accepting that Congress can't get anything done that would protect the American people from financial ruin, much as they still collect their pay and benefits for life. What is wrong with this picture?

If the United States were a brand, would we know what it stands for? For many people around the world we are decadence, laziness, cold self-interest, profit at all costs, immoral, lax, overweight and indebted. How is that a brand we can feel good about? Would you hire an employee who projected those attributes as their brand? It's time for us to take a long hard look at what we are doing, whether we are not taking care of our health, or our employees, or our world interests. It's time to stop texting and multitasking, and start paying attention to the brand that we project to the world.

The United States is a very generous country, always lending a helping hand, with a fist full of dollars. This has not won us any acclaim: the very countries we assist turn around and try to hurt us. Maybe we should curtail our aid. There are certainly enough impoverished people here at home. Would this diminish our brand? Or is it so diminished already that it wouldn't make a difference?

We are nearing an election which promises to be a close one with a nation deeply divided. We are also undecided: no one wants to relive the last four years, but can we trust what the Romney/Ryan team has in store for us? The one thing we must ask ourselves as we move towards Nov. 6th is: will it make a difference? We can only hope that our American brand will re-assert itself in a positive way; that we will start taking care of the basics and rallying around concepts like honesty, integrity, hard work. Now those are brand pillars that could make us the shining light to those less fortunate that we once were.

Marylou P. Kay

51. DIGGING UP YOUR DIGITAL DIRT

With the elections behind us, we run head-on into a military scandal of far-reaching proportions. And rather than chuckle at the foibles of those on high, we hang our heads with shame. The military is expected to be beyond reproach. But here is the pathos of the situation: General David Petreus, a well-respected military figure with a lifetime of achievements and service to the country, has given up his career due to his indiscretion. It is tragic. Adding to the surreal situation is the possibility that General John Allen could be implicated in a similar situation with socialite Jill Kelley.

In 2006, David Petreus met Paula Broadwell while lecturing at Harvard. Studying at the Kennedy School of Government, Broadwell approached the General about her research interests. In 2008, enrolled as a doctoral student at Kings College London, she started writing her dissertation on Petreus and his leadership style. This entailed several interviews with him. Petreus moved to U.S. Central Command in late 2008 only to be taken out in June 2010 to replace General Stanley McChrystal relieved of command in Afghanistan due to comments made in an interview with Rolling Stone magazine. Petreus retired from the Army in August 2011 and became Director of the CIA in September 2011. It is supposedly around this time that the affair begins. By June of 2012, the two agree to part ways. The public would never have known if it were not for the anonymous emails sent to Jill Kelley, a family friend, warning her to stay away from Petreus. Ms. Kelley called an FBI agent, Frederick Humphries, a personal friend, and the ensuing investigation brought to light the extramarital relationship between Petreus and Broadwell.

There are countless emails, text messages, phone calls exchanged between the parties under investigation. Even the friendship between Kelley and Humphries has a cyber-half-life, as if it were some radioactive material that doesn't go away. And that is the point, nothing you do on the internet, on Facebook, in emails and texts ever goes away. Even if you delete things, they can be traced and tracked. This is the core lesson of safeguarding our personal brand: once it is on the internet, it will stay there forever.

This means we have to take great care in what we post and although we do not think about these things, we must start being accountable for what is out there. Like a pervasive credit rating or a bad reference, it follows you around. Think before you write an email or a text. The old rule with emails still holds: "Don't put anything in an email that you would be hesitant to put in a newspaper". Yet with all of our blogs and groups, we forget that we are on a very public stage and that whatever small thing we put out there, will be captured by a search engine only to show up when we least expect it. You can no longer count on the anonymity of the masses.

Career counselors often advise us to clean up our digital dirt, but it is almost impossible to make changes once something is out there. A little like the Recall Message feature in Outlook, it calls more attention to you when you attempt to cancel out what you've already written. We have already seen employers asking for Facebook passwords. We live in an age of too much information and since there is no regulation in the way of full disclosure, we have to start exercising some self-discipline in what we will express publicly. Most likely we mortals will not be involved in a scandal of the magnitude we have witnessed recently. But would you want to have some doubts about how you represent yourself? Better keep your own counsel, "discretion is the better part of valor", and take charge of your digital reputation, it is the core of your personal brand.

52. PAULA DEEN'S BRAND:
GONE BABY, GONE

The recent Paula Deen debacle shows us how fragile our personal brand can be. We work so hard to build up a brand to be proud of. We make good business decisions; craft our public persona to be something that will gain the world's attention. But at the end of it all, we are human beings, we make mistakes, we cannot live up to the ideals we have set up for ourselves.

In the circumstances surrounding Ms. Deen, she could not have known thirty years ago that her words would be taken out of context on a future date. Recently when glibly discussing plans for a dinner party like those held in the antebellum south, she couldn't have known that once again her comments on the elegance of those times would be taken out of context. But in these mean spirited days of political correctness, people are looking for every flaw, every careless word in order to make a point, win a lawsuit, perhaps gain a monetary settlement through destroying the livelihood of another.

In these so very correct times, people still only care about themselves. Recently I had a flat tire and with the help of Triple

A, was 'rescued'. While commenting about how the Triple A Operator asks if you are in a safe place (which I was at the time), Jim explained to me that just two weeks ago he had a call from a person who said they were not in a safe place and asked to be given the highest priority, the top of the list of those needing help. The lady in question was parked in front of a police station. Jim's other call was from a young mother stranded in a car on the side of the highway with two infant children on a hot day. Fortunately, Jim had his priorities straight: he stopped for the young mother before continuing on to the woman at the police station arriving 45 minutes behind schedule. When he explained why, the person responded "I don't know that woman or her children; I don't care about them. I was supposed to have the highest priority on the list!"

It is dismaying to see Paula Deen's empire disappear without a trace. Her book is being removed from the shelves; her cookware line will be allowed to sell out and then not re-stocked. Her shows are canceled. For someone in the public eye, it can't get any worse. Even if you didn't enjoy her style of cooking, you almost have to cringe thinking how it is not fair. And there are many who do feel that this ostracism is much greater that what the transgression requires. Yet there are many who are unscathed when caught up in similar turmoil. It is hard to determine what lies at the heart of this duality. Why can someone like Alec Baldwin get away with using derogatory language, and Paula Deen cannot? He made his offensive tweets a couple of days ago, Deen's comments go back decades. Perhaps we have come to expect more of Paula Deen, whereas with Alec Baldwin, we are unfazed by controversy, it's nothing new to him. Whatever the reasons, we can only hope that there is some hopeful resolution, all while knowing that with a personal brand overnight it can be gone, baby gone.

VI THE WRAP UP

A brand is an identifying mark, a trademark, something that conveys the identity of the bearer. A personal brand is your identity, your mark. It's what people will remember about you, what you stand for, what you aspire to. Your personal brand is a way to distinguish yourself from others, from the competition. It's a way to take what is intrinsically you and use it for strategic advantage. For all these reasons it's imperative that you develop your own unique brand and that you learn to communicate it to the world you live in, and perhaps the world at large.

Nowadays we are all a bit bigger that we can conceptualize. The internet and social media have achieved this for us. We can no longer develop our little personal brand in a vacuum, but rather set it out there for the world to see and react to it.

What we find is that people are reacting to that brand all the time. They probably reacted to it before we knew we had a brand. So as long as it's out there, let's make sure it reflects us just the way we are or the way we want it to be. And that is why we read about brands, we understand them; we look at the brands of others and make decisions as to what will define us. We examine the brands of exemplars, people we look up to. We also take a peek at brands that we do not envy and wonder how these people came to mean these things that are not so positive. It can't be helped, we are blessed with curiosity, and we want to understand the world out there. We also want to express ourselves in a way that is true to our inner being. So we investigate ways to get at what makes us original, unique, memorable. Hopefully we come up with some ideas by observing not only the world, but how we react to it.

In this book we have reviewed different brands and commented on them. We have recommended ways to develop what you have and take it to the next level, ways to showcase your special attributes and build on your dreams. We have included tips on networking, job search, interviewing and presenting yourself to the world. There are many ways to get to the heart of that brand incorporating your interests, dreams, skills, abilities.

You can take a walk through emotional intelligence, defining job types, management styles, or just by deciding how you do not want to be represented. We've also learned that because we live in a time of social media, of Google, Bing, Ask, Facebook, LinkedIn, we have many tools to display our brand. But they are vehicles; we must retain our responsibility as the designated driver of our brand. We cannot take it lightly and must think carefully before posting information.

We have all seen where this openness can lead us, it is powerful. We can only hope that this power inspires you in a way that leads you to step out of the uniformity of job seekers and into the special group of brand aware individuals who are facing their destiny one challenge at a time.

ABOUT THE AUTHOR

Marylou Ponzi Kay is the founder and president of MPK Associates, a human resources consultancy launched after an extensive career working at such companies as American Express, Benetton, Canon, Esselte Pendaflex, JP Morgan, Smartmatic and Melia Resort Hotels. Her practice centers on Human Resources and Cross Cultural Communications. Marylou consults for a wide variety of firms including biotechnology, electronics manufacturing, air cargo, international restaurant chain and global relocation services provider. She is passionate about intercultural communications and personal branding.

Formerly an adjunct Professor in Human Resources at Florida International University, New York Institute of Technology, and most recently Southeastern College where she created the curriculum for a Human Resources Associates Degree program.

Marylou serves on the board of the Greater Miami Society for Human Resources Management and the Back on Track Network for Job Search. Marylou earned Master's Degrees from the University of Iowa, and from the State University of New York at Buffalo. In addition, Marylou earned certification in Labor and Industrial Relations from the New York Institute of Technology. She is fluent in Spanish, French and Italian. Her website is www.mpkassociates.com

www.ingramcontent.com/pod-product-compliance
Lightning Source LLC
Chambersburg PA
CBHW051315170526
45166CB00002B/547